Live INSIDE OUT

Sarah Smith

TRILOGY
A WHOLLY OWNED SUBSIDIARY OF **TBN**
PROFESSIONAL PUBLISHING MEETS POWERFUL PROMOTION

Live Inside Out

Trilogy Christian Publishers

A Wholly Owned Subsidiary of Trinity Broadcasting Network

2442 Michelle Drive, Tustin, CA 92780

Copyright © 2024 by S. Smith

All Scripture quotations are taken from the Holy Bible, New International Version®, NIV®. Copyright © 1973, 1978, 1984, 2011 by Biblica, Inc. TM Used by permission of Zondervan. All rights reserved worldwide. www.zondervan.com. The "NIV" and "New International Version" are trademarks registered in the United States Patent and Trademark Office by Biblica, Inc.TM

All rights reserved, including the right to reproduce this book or portions thereof in any form whatsoever.

For information, address Trilogy Christian Publishing

Rights Department, 2442 Michelle Drive, Tustin, Ca 92780.

Trilogy Christian Publishing/TBN and colophon are trademarks of Trinity Broadcasting Network.

For information about special discounts for bulk purchases, please contact Trilogy Christian Publishing.

Trilogy Disclaimer: The views and content expressed in this book are those of the author and may not necessarily reflect the views and doctrine of Trilogy Christian Publishing or the Trinity Broadcasting Network.

10 9 8 7 6 5 4 3 2 1

Library of Congress Cataloging-in-Publication Data is available.

ISBN 979-8-89333-640-5

ISBN 979-8-89333-641-2 (ebook)

Dedication

To my husband, Shane, who gave me the pink Bible. To my son, Slade, and my daughter, Lyndee, who introduced me to Jesus and brought me away from religion. This book is all about the truths I have uncovered and the beautiful simplicity of a relationship with Jesus. It had to be just me and Jesus first. Let these words bring others to the same beautiful place of freedom that our family now knows we have within us.

Table of Contents

Introduction..........7

Renew Your Mind..........11

Know Who He Is..........21

See Yourself as He Sees You..........43

Use Your Authority..........63

See It..........77

Thank Him..........105

Just Be Loved..........111

Invitation..........119

Introduction

This book is for everyone. Truly come as you are and read. Jesus is for everyone, and He is the only way. He is the only door that leads to life. Jesus is the story. He is the solution, not you. We are made to be the receiver, not the achiever. You can only get water if you have something to receive it in. We can only receive Him, who is the living water, if we are a willing receiver. Religion and works are not it. We end up building the wall ourselves that blocks the water from flowing. It is all about what He did, not what you did wrong or do right now. You are loved and a treasure. Accepting Jesus as our Savior is simply through faith and acknowledgment that He did it, not you. We all must first know we need his saving grace. Are you a whosoever or a whoever? Yes, you are, and so am I. Praise God! "For God so loved the world that he gave his one and only Son, that whoever believes in him shall not perish but have eternal life in him" (John 3:16). This is you and me.

Have you ever thought about the words "I am what I say I am"? How about the words "I will do what I say I will do"? This is powerful because words have power. God used words to bring everything into existence. The truth in His Word is what everything stands upon. If His Word were not true, everything would cease to exist. The only way the words we use will be a positive driving force in our lives is to know who God really is, not the false image that has been handed down from generation to generation. I felt a gentle hand guiding me to write this book so the amazing truths that I now know have been inside of me since I accepted Jesus in my heart at ten years old could be shared. These truths are in every born-again believer. I am now starting to grasp the beautiful gifts I have been freely given. My prayer is that these words show you, not just tell you, what you need to do. I speak it over everyone.

To be born-again is to accept Jesus Christ and, therefore, be saved. He paid for all our sins once and for all. When we are saved by Him, we are given a brand-new perfect spirit that He freely shares with all who believe. The key to receiving everything Jesus already provided is to notice that we must accept Him. This is a big reminder to understand that we have free will. Therefore, we must make a choice to receive the gift. Receiving Jesus is simply that. I just wanted to share for anyone who has not really heard much about receiving Jesus as your Savior that you may hear it said as getting saved, getting born-again (meaning receiving a brand-new spirit, just like Jesus's spirit), or accepting Jesus in your heart.

Life is found in our innermost part, our spirit. Yes, we all have a spirit, not just a soul. Our spirit is made new again, full of life, perfect, and righteous no longer corrupted by sin through accepting Jesus as our Savior. We have three parts: spirit, soul, and body. God is also three parts, Father, Son, and Holy Spirit. Life is given to us to live from our innermost part, our spirit, not our body (flesh). Instead, we are taught by worldly standards to live from our outermost part, our body, to the point we are taught that our body rules us. To find life for the very first time in truth is to live in this world inside out. To truly live is to live backward from the way the world does. Living by the spirit is the only way to find life, and this life only comes from God through Jesus. The finished work of Jesus makes this possible because He provided our redemption from sin. God is a spirit, and He made us in His image in spirit. Life in the spirit is freedom. Life from the body first is bondage to sin and death. Life from the spirit unites us. Life from the flesh divides us. Our spirit is life-giving. Our soul is our personality and feelings. Our body is our shell, a system that God gave us to serve us, not rule us. There is godly servitude, which is love, joy, and life forever. Our body is a system that was created to work correctly for us and serve us in our godly purpose. Money is also a worldly system, not a God system. Money is also supposed to serve us in our godly purpose and is not to rule us. We are not to serve our body, money, or anything else but God. All things, including our bodies, listen to the authority and power that is in the name of Jesus. He is our Savior and redeemer. We are given His authority when we are born again. That is something that we all must know to see the victory we have in Jesus, the relationship we have back with God because of what Jesus did for us all.

God's kingdom is built upon and motivated by love and love only. It is not based upon anything with you or me besides just being loved by Him. That is one huge revelation. This means it has nothing to do with what we have done, do now, or will in the future. That is why it took one perfect sacrifice one time motivated by love that is Jesus. While I have been walking in this awareness, I could receive what God had already provided that is just waiting for us all. God showed me seven blessings that we have the ability and free will to walk in to not lose sight of the truth of God and His love for every one of us. These seven gifts will be shared throughout the book. This will help us to focus on Jesus and his forever foundation to God and not one we try to build ourselves that will surely fall. I pray you receive the blessings, too, and come to a place of living for God through Jesus, where we belong in the kingdom mindset and not the ways of the world any longer.

This book is subtitled "The Greatest Awakening" because we first need transformation within ourselves before we can share it with others and see a lasting change. It takes knowing that God is the author of love and life. The enemy is the leader of destruction and confusion. Jesus said to go and make disciples. He did not say go and make converts. A disciple follows the Teacher, Jesus, is changed by Him, and is now one committed to His finished work. A convert receives the gift but does not share and produce spiritual "fruit" or abundance. The true change is in self, not just being shared between large groups of people and thinking that is it. It is first the change in self and then to share this with others. What Jesus does for us individually is our testimony to share with others. We do not want to just have converts waiting for Jesus to come back. We want disciples. The goal of this writing is to show you, not just tell you, what I have found and how to receive it, too. He has changed my life, and He will absolutely change yours. This is not for the other person. He is for you, too.

Renew Your Mind

God made us to live from the deepest level, our spirit. We were not made to live from the surface. The surface has no strength, no root to sustain life and stand strong. To live from the inside out is to live from our spirit. This is a kingdom mindset. It is the opposite of the world. Living in a kingdom mindset is living for God. Live life inside out to find it. We are to live from our spirit, soul, then body not our body (flesh) first. In this fallen world, we are first aware of our flesh, and that is what we live by. If the truth of God's Word is not shared with us, we do not know to live by our spirit. Living with a kingdom mindset means not just going along with the world. It means to choose Jesus, not self. However, there is an adjustment just like a pitcher must be able to adjust to many factors in baseball, like the weather, batter's approach, and umpire calls. The adjustment is inside us first, and remember it starts with Jesus, not self. He provided the means back to God. The adjustment in us is letting what He gave us be used. It is like if we move to a completely different state from where we grew up, we need time to get to know our surroundings, and then after a while, it becomes home. So it is when we are born again. We get to know our true identity for the first time and get to know what we have in Christ. We are now as close to home as we will ever be until we are right next to Jesus. Through Him, we are righteous ground and must learn and adjust to expect great things and not settle for defeat. The approach to people and situations must be adjusted depending on what is at the forefront. The thing that does not change is one has to remember God is the only giver of life, and we know not what we do until we have Christ. That is the blessing to move forward with Jesus and understand that someone else may not see what you see now or even display what the world calls common courtesy for human beings. This is because without God, standards just keep falling, and destruction is definite. We must be loved and approach people and situations from a place of love and rest that God has already provided. That is the kingdom mindset. He does not need our help. He needs us to be usable. One of the hardest things I have ever done is realize this and just rest. I do not want anyone else to suffer like I have in my life. Please know that God does not either. I still waiver but what matters is I cannot lose what I have, and I am always brought right back to where I should be. Jesus gave us His spirit once and for all. "Whoever is united with the Lord is one with Him in spirit" (1 Corinthians 6:17). He shared what He had with us. We have it forever.

When we accept Jesus in our hearts, we receive what He has freely shared: a perfect spirit. We are then made to be the righteousness of God in Christ. Our spirit is perfect. The rest of the walk is the renewing of our mind, so our spirit flows out into our soul, body (flesh), and then to others. We have the Son, who is the door to God. This brings us back to God, where we belong. We then have our Heavenly Father forever. God is so good that we are given His Spirit within us through the work of Jesus, which is the Holy Spirit to guide and teach us. We must welcome the Holy Spirit to teach and guide us in this world. If we do not, we will just live saved, going to heaven, having eternal life, and still go on living by our own guidance, which will just lead us to more hardship in this world. This does not allow us to walk in all His blessings now. Just as God never forced and did provide free will, it is the same with the Holy Spirit. We must submit our will to the Holy Spirit also by welcoming Him to guide our lives after we accept Jesus in our hearts. Once we accept Jesus in our hearts, the Holy Spirit is waiting and willing but will not lead our lives until we welcome Him to do so. That is love. God's will is never forced. When we invite the Holy Spirit to lead our lives, we walk in acknowledgment that we now have the Father, the Son, and the Holy Spirit. We freely have the ability to use all spiritual blessings that came from Jesus. Yes, when we are born again, we have this, but it is the same as not having something if we just walk around not knowing what we have or do not put it to use. The Holy Spirit helps us with this. That is what Jesus meant when He said to "go and make disciples of all nations, baptizing them in the name of the Father, and of the Son, and of the Holy Spirit" (Matthew 28:19). He was not talking about water baptism. He was saying go share the good news so others can have what you have and share the baptism of the Holy Spirit to guide and teach them along the way. Jesus asked the disciples to stay until He ascended to heaven, and God sent the Holy Spirit because they could not and should not spread the good news of the gospel alone. Not one person should try to do this because this is how truth even accidentally gets changed or left out of the gift that we are free to receive from Jesus.

    The Lord blesses us before we even do anything. Our sins were paid for by Jesus before we even lived to commit any. He blesses us first before we even start walking to know Him. Everything is there. We just reach out and receive it when we make Jesus our Lord and Savior. We open the door to eternal life. Jesus gives us a new perfect spirit provided by Him being the one and only perfect sacrifice for our sins once and for all. This is what it means to be born again. So truly, He blessed us even before we asked for His saving grace. Sin was dealt with before we sinned. It took one sin, the very first sin, to corrupt everyone and everything. So it took one perfect sacrifice, Jesus, one time, to atone for our sins forever. Our walk is receiving a new spirit that has eternal life and is blessed because we have freedom and redemption from sin. We can live with God now and be forever redeemed from all that sin brought to this fallen world.

When we are saved, we are redeemed from sin and are drawn away from it. We cannot save ourselves. The Old Testament has so many accounts of people God used who tried to get God to move when they just had to trust Him. It was God doing the good, not them. Sin cannot be a source of good. They were intended to be blessed and a means for Him to work through since God is a spirit. There is an account in Judges 11 of someone saying to God that he would give the first thing that came through his door when he returned home safely as a burnt offering if God would provide victory over their current enemy. All this man had to do was trust. God said move, so his response was to move, not cast lots and bargain with God. So, because of what he said, the first thing that came through his door was his only child, a daughter. He kept his word, and his daughter died because of it. Do you think that was God's plan? Absolutely not. He was and is never willing for any to perish.

We should not, even with good intent, try to help out God or try to take the place that only Jesus could fill. It will return void. Sin cannot pay for sin or provide anything good. Until we are saved, we are a source of sin, not righteousness. When we get saved, our spirit is made brand-new and perfect, just like Jesus. The issue is we are not taught what we have, so it is like we live as if we do not have it. We make it all about us and what we did or need to do to fix things. Jesus paid for our sins before we had any. When we accept Jesus in our lives, the door is no longer shut to God. It is about accepting the key to the door, not God dealing with your sins.

The door is already there. Sin for all of us was dealt with on the cross. Saving grace and eternal life have been provided to all also. We must choose it because we have free will. "Seek and you will find" (Matthew 7:7). Jesus says this with a promise. He is for everyone. The thing to remember is you must ask. He will not force or just come without an invitation from you. The key is your heart, and Jesus is the door to God. Our hearts have to either be with God or with the world. Your heart cannot be in two places. We are only to give our hearts and worship God.

Eternal life starts as soon as we accept Jesus in our hearts. We need the baptism of the Holy Spirit to guide us in the fullness of what Jesus provided. We must welcome the Holy Spirit to guide our lives. He will not force us. It is important to remember Jesus conquered death. Through Him, there is only eternal life to experience. Only when we have the love and peace God provided through Jesus will we have that with others who share this truth. It is first the renewing of our mind that brings an awakening to who God is and what Jesus did then, we can truly love others. If this were not true, we would not be hearing that we are in or need a Third Great Awakening. Until the greatest awakening in oneself, we do not realize that everything is already done. Our only thing to do is receive it by faith and rest in the finished work of Jesus. All of us have an innate ability to know what we truly need. We just run from it mainly because it seems too good to be true or does not make sense to our logic. In the flesh, we think we have to earn everything. The flesh is also prideful and wants credit and recognition for everything. Our worth is not found in our achievements. It is found in Jesus.

To live by the spirit with Jesus is to live completely relying on what He did for us. It is also completely relying on the Holy Spirit's guidance, not our own. We must live inside out from the way the world lives. The world is all about feelings (soul) and flesh (physical body). Many of us do not even know we have a spirit because soul and spirit are interchanged in the world when the two are totally separate parts of us. The two are not the same at all. God is a spirit who made us to live in spirit with Him. We are to live by our born-again spirit first then the goodness of Jesus pours out into our soul and body and then to others. It is our spirit that became brand-new just like Jesus. He shared His spirit with us, and we are one with Him and make up the body of Christ through His shared spirit. This is why Christ unites us with God, and then we are united with other Christ followers because we have the same truly identical spirit, a spirit of love and peace. We are made to each bring a part that makes the whole body work.

Our soul (personality and feelings) and our body (flesh) are not brand-new yet. We cannot go to these parts to look for change first. The change was in our deepest part, the main part and only source of life, our spirit. We will receive our glorified bodies that are perfect, just like Jesus, when He returns. Then and only then will our minds and bodies know all things. Right now, the born-again believer has all this in their spirit. We live by our spirit in faith by reading and living by God's Word, the Bible. His Word is our instructions for living on this earth right now in its corrupted state. Right now, we know all things in our spirit. We have the mind of Christ in our spirit right now as believers (1 Corinthians 2:16).

We are to let the perfection of our spirit pour out into our souls, bodies, and others to live now on this earth with all the benefits that Jesus made available and the perfect spirit He gave us. As He sits at the right hand of the Father, so are believers in this world (1 John 4:14). We have access to all good things through our spirits. When we receive our glorified bodies, then they will be known to all parts of us. Our minds will not be trying to do something different from our spirits. The spirit is the source and has all power. Our soul, which is our personality, feelings, and thoughts, has to be renewed to what we have in Christ right now. This is the renewing of our minds. If we do not renew our minds to what we have and who we now are, then there is no harvest. We go to heaven, and that is it. However, if we renew our minds as God says to, there will always be an abundant harvest now and forever. After we are born-again, the walk becomes renewing our mind in His Word so our soul aligns with our spirit and not our body (flesh), which is sinful in this fallen, corrupted state of the world right now. Our soul is in the middle of our spirit and body. We have to choose what it aligns with by renewing our minds and sharing this with others. To live now in all blessings, our soul must be in agreement with our perfect spirit, not our flesh. To believe with all of our hearts is to have our souls in agreement with our spirits. Then and only then the righteousness and blessings can pour out into our bodies.

Believing with all of our hearts is not measured in worldly terms as to a certain amount, it is simply a choice, a union of our spirit and soul to becoming just that much closer to Christ. I used to think I had to believe with a certain amount of faith because I thought it was about what I do and not what Jesus did. Because I did not know, I would try to use worldly measures for godly things. It will never work because the things of this world are not the things of God until the earth is made brand-new again when Jesus comes back. Just as we must choose to accept Christ, so do we have to choose to live by our spirit in Christ from then on out. The flesh is still corrupt and is attracted to the corrupted world. Choose the spirit and have the victory. Jesus provided this; He fought the battle so that you do not have to. Just receive the finished work and live with the peace of God.

The Bible says whosoever or whoever. Praise God, I am a whosoever, and so are you! Give your life to Christ, and you will find it for the first time. God's Word is true and never fails or returns void. He is so good and only desires our hearts. I felt I should read the Bible to my children when I was expecting them. I had no reason to do this. God is clear and gets the glory. The Bible was never read to me, and I was told to not touch the Bible that was on our shelf that I just felt a pull to at about seven years old. I listened with such peace when God said read to my children. I read a children's Bible. The blessing was for all of us. I learned, and my children were hearing God's Word even in the womb. Please know God's Word is His, and it never changes, lies, and will never return void. If it is easier at first, start with a children's Bible. It blessed me, and I know it will bless you. My children and I each read through it ten to twelve times before they grew to ask for more. The goodness of God and His Word brings life and love.

My children heard His Word from the beginning and then later were the ones who brought me to really know Jesus. That is my testimony. Since I was only taught religion, I just kept trying to reach God and earn my way to Him. I knew He was there, yet I felt so far away. Then, through my children's journey, they brought me to Jesus, who is the door to God. I had been saved at ten years old, but I did not know what I had. There was not anyone around me sharing who He is and what I now had. I knew I was changed from that moment. I just did not know how or what changed in me. I did not know I had a spirit until about six years ago. At first, my children did not even realize what they were doing or what they had done for me. So, I am here to tell you God uses anyone who is willing; no one is unqualified in the kingdom of God. He worked through my greatest blessing on earth, my children.

We must renew our minds with God's Word because we are not born with truth or always taught this truth. We do not see and witness what the generations before us did, so it is so important to share (1 Timothy 4:1–16). Many of us have heard actions speak louder than words. Well, when we renew our minds, we realize this is not so. Words are just as important as actions. And none of it will be good without Jesus and knowing we are loved because of Him. Actions can be false representations of people because those who are hurting and just want love oftentimes just are not nice. See the false display here. Words are powerful and are how everything was created. Even the commercials that come on TV are mostly about problems or fear. So, we just grow up thinking we are supposed to have problems. No, absolutely not. We are intended to live beyond circumstances. For example, if you do not like your job but do not seem to find another, take the opportunity to trust that if you let God, He will turn everything around for good. A boss can only control your life if you let them. If you are born again, then you are in the world, not of it. I hear so many believers living in the Old Testament. Hear this—*Old*! I used to live there in defeat.

We are and were intended to be living in the new covenant, the New Testament. We are meant to live expecting good things, not bad, nor planning for negative circumstances. This world functions on this and what ifs. When we trust God and let Him lead our lives, we are living in true safety. We are then walking responsibly because God does not miss things; we do. The Old Testament is shared so we can know what we now have in Jesus. We are given the past of the Old Testament, so we do not continue to repeat it. The Old Testament is full of repeated unfortunate cycles. This happens in families over and over. We are not to stay in the old but be in the new. This is another reason why we renew our minds. We are not to be focused on religious traditions. Many who think they are going to heaven because they believe in God will not. They will not see the kingdom then but will also miss all the blessings now if they do not accept our one and only Savior, Jesus Christ. He is the only door. He is the narrow door because we cannot get in it, boasting and being full of ourselves in works and comparisons. Come to the end of self to find your true self in Jesus. We must be saved through Jesus and His work, not our own. Not one person can save themselves. What matters is we accept Him and receive eternal life now and forever. Jesus made that clear. "Indeed there are those who are last who will be first, and first who will be last" (Luke 13:30). All that matters is we come to Him.

Religious traditions are why Jesus was put on the cross. He conquered sin and made it clear religion is a wall between God and us. People had made even the law all about them and lived in self-righteousness instead of admitting they could not do it and needed to be saved. Jesus spoke about the traditions of even eating certain foods. He said that it is not what goes in a person that defiles them. It is what comes out of their hearts. This is when He declared all food clean (Mark 7:18–19). We are not to call anything wrong or impure that God has declared otherwise (Acts 10:15). We are not supposed to be distracted by all kinds of teachings and works. Our hearts are strengthened only through grace, not by what we eat, practice, or good deeds we think we do. Jesus brings the good deeds because He makes us good. We cannot try to be good. Good is in Jesus. Just like when Jesus walked on this earth, the very ones sharing the law were the very ones not following it (Hebrews 13:9–10). Jesus is the only way to goodness, which is God. Eating only certain foods takes us right back to before Jesus came, like He did not do anything at all. He did! We should not walk backward, so do not move that way. What our minds are staying upon is where we will be. If we are focused on God and living in the spirit, it is life, peace, and joy. If we are focused on the world and the flesh, it is confusion, destruction, and death. I have heard accounts of people being stranded somewhere with no food and some even injured. They survived against all odds. When they were asked why, the answer was usually stated as they refused to die. A mind set on life and faith that they will make it even if one is not aware of it is just that—faith. It is not in our own strength. Life prevails when we do not limit God by our circumstances. God's love brings life and also brings us beyond circumstances.

Know Who He Is

Renewing our minds leads to knowing who God is. Yes, He is the one true sovereign God. This simply means He is all-powerful. However, please catch this: He gave us free will from the beginning. He is love and desires our love. God willingly gave us the power to choose. If He did not, we would have no choice in anything. The truth is our life is full of choices. Only one choice leads to life and that is through Jesus. Love is never forced, or it is not love. If we did not have a choice in things or influence over circumstances, everyone would be saved and have eternal life. There would be no problems because God is good. If He chose to use His sovereignty completely, everything would crumble. His Word is truth and what everything stands upon. His Word says we have free will. If God went against this, all creation would cease to exist. He is perfect love, and His Word is truth. He possesses all power but does not choose to use it all because He is love. The thing we have to realize is that bad things happen, but it is not from God. He will turn things around for good. He does not bring anything bad. Jesus finished everything. God's wrath against sin was satisfied through the work of Jesus, and atonement was provided. We now have peace with God. Even when peace was not there between us and God because of the wrath of sin, He still loved, protected, and provided. Again, God's Word is truth, and He is perfection. There had to be punishment for sin. It was automatic because God is good, and sin is evil. Good and evil cannot exist as one together. There is and has to be a separation. That is why sin brings punishment. God wants our hearts and nothing else.

One thousand years is like one day to God. God is forever young, big in love, and not scary. Because of what Jesus did, we have the opportunity to have an eye-to-eye close relationship with Him. He is not looking down at us. He says to come boldly. He is Peace, Perfect Father, and Forever Friend. He is forever young, and so are we through Jesus. Just look at the horse. A horse is so strong and powerful, yet so gentle. A horse just wants your heart. That is just how God is and has always been and will forever be. God does not like pride because it is destructive always. Someone riding a horse all about themselves and in pride tends to end up on the ground as we do when we live in pride throughout our lives. We end up falling and failing. This world will say take pride and be prideful. Pride goes before destruction, a superior attitude before a fall (Proverbs 16:8). To love God is to dislike evil (Proverbs 8:13). Grace is free. It is the only free gift, and this is provided through Jesus. There is no trace of pride in that. We cannot explain why we receive grace in any other way besides the only reason is love. The key is remembering it has nothing to do with us or our efforts. Everyone who trusts is blessed by grace. Therefore, there is no place for pride because pride is being about self not Jesus. It is Jesus who submitted to God's will. If He had pride, we would still have death. The glory goes to God. Faith is receiving this gift of grace and believing it (Hebrews 11:1).

God is the voice of reason. He is what makes everything work peacefully and as He created it to function. When sin entered the world and separated us from God, Jesus came so we could have Him back and receive the one true voice of reason within us. I saw Jesus in the word "reason." This word represents the flowing of the Son in us. "Rea" means flowing. Jesus is the Son of God who shares His perfect spirit full of life-giving water. Everything stands on God's spoken

Word. He spoke everything into creation. His Word is His spoken Word, and it is peace. His voice is like the sound of flowing waves. This is the reason that the flow of water is such a peaceful sound. When we are born again, we receive His voice of reason. We should not walk toward conflict. If we do, we will immediately know that it is not the place for us and have to turn from it. When God leads us, there is peace even beyond negative circumstances. One cannot argue like they once did. We are pulled from that behavior. We are called to be peacemakers and problem solvers because that is what Jesus did for us. The way we do that is to share Jesus in our words and our actions. Jesus provided peace between us and God. He solved all of our problems. We are to share that same gift of opportunity with others. Peace only comes from God. We have that because of Jesus. It is peace with Him and then peace with others who have that same peace with Him through Jesus. Peace among men only comes from each of us having Jesus in our hearts. God is good. Jesus makes the way, the drawing to good and not evil. He leads us away from sin. This is something we will not do on our own ever. Let us remember to not be led by our feelings but by the love of Christ within us in our spirits. Any opportunity is a chance to share Christ with others.

    The true gospel being preached is about Jesus and what He provided, not you and not your works. Catch it, please—not about you. We miss that. Andrew Wommack taught me that God loves me. He also taught me that I have a spirit, soul, and body. I only knew of soul and body. The Bible says God is a spirit. We are made in His image in spirit. It is the first and most important piece, the life-giving part. Our soul and body (our flesh) follow that truth when we live by our spirits. We see so many people thinking that nothing changed when they received Jesus as their Savior because many do not even know they have a spirit. They do not even know that they have the main part that we are to live by with God. It is our spirit that became brand-new and just like Jesus when we were born again. The rest of the walk is renewing our mind to what we have in our spirit and that pouring out into our souls and then bodies. To live by the body (flesh) is death. To live by the spirit is life (Romans 8:5–6). Joseph Prince taught me that God loves me and wants to bless me first and foremost. That is it. It is grace. This is not earned; it is given freely. I am the righteousness of God in Christ. This means I am made right and sinless before God because of Jesus's shed blood. Throughout all time, God has blessed us before anything else. He provides always and always has done so despite our choices. God made everything that has breath to praise Him. Mark 6:15 says to go and share the news with all creation. Wow, what an eye-opener of His love. He wants nothing to suffer but to be blessed. He said all creation. We are to care for all creation, not dominate it. His Word is a seed that will produce a harvest every time and never run out. His Word clothes and covers us with warmth.

Sin entered the world through Adam. This put a barrier between God and us. The barrier was our spirit no longer had life. We became dominated by our flesh, which brought bondage to sin. Eve was the first one who disobeyed. However, it was Adam's sin that caused the fall. Where there is sin, there can be no righteousness. Good turns to bad. If the foundation is bad, the whole thing is bad. We need our Savior, Jesus Christ, to make our spirit brand-new, perfect, and righteous once and for all. He is the good foundation. We do not accept Jesus for our sins to be forgiven. We think too much about ourselves. Sin was already paid for by Jesus, not us. When we accept Jesus, we are receiving what He did, and the part that we still need is to have a brand-new born-again spirit, perfect and righteous, just like His, to have our bond with God back as He intended. Our part is to receive that new perfect spirit that is no longer corrupted by sin. God cannot dwell among sin. As it took one sin to corrupt the world and our spirit, it took one perfect sacrifice, Jesus, one time to redeem us all, once and forever. We are to turn to God, not away, and be one with Jesus forever in our perfect born-again spirit and reunited with God through this that Jesus did. He changes our nature. It is only changed through Jesus. It cannot be changed without Him.

On our own, we just continue living in a fallen state. It is just like my bird dog will not stop chasing birds even though a glass window stops her. It is her nature in this world. A horse is always looking out for predators no matter how domesticated and safe they are because sin in the world has brought fear to all creation. Predator and prey mentality are the nature of animals in this world. This occurred when the fall happened, and animals turned on one another. When Jesus comes back, this will no longer be the case. Jesus changes our nature now to life and peace from death and despair. Then, the saved share this peace with all creation right here and now.

Adam was created first, and he had firsthand information from God. Humans are made in His image. It was the first human's sin that corrupted our spirit, and the world fell to sin because God's Word is truth and what all creation stands upon. Righteousness and sin cannot exist together. God is always giving and merciful. He sent Adam and Eve out of the Garden of Eden so that they would not live forever in a fallen evil state and suffer forever without Him. God could not dwell with them any longer because sin came, and He cannot dwell amongst evil. God clothed them and sent them away to somewhere else out of mercy. This was again pointing to the fact that we would all need Jesus to save us from an eternity of punishment because of being born into sin and corrupted by it. Another account of mercy is Noah being spared even though everything had become just evil. Noah put his faith in God and did what He said no matter what others thought or said. He was building an ark, which is a boat, in a time when there was no rain and everything was dry. He trusted in God's Word, not the opinions of other people who did not know what God knew. He told Noah that there would be a flood to wipe out all of the people and animals that were not in the ark.

No one outside of Noah knew about it because he was the one who trusted God. Noah survived only because he trusted God. It was not until Moses was given the law with the sole purpose of showing us our sin that sin would be imputed to people. Once we are aware of something, we have a responsibility to choose God, not the world. Sin was not imputed for so many years after sin entered the world through Adam until the law was given. God's intention is never to destroy but to give life abundantly. Without Christ, people are evil and will do bad things and fail every time. All need Jesus. There is no in-between.

We have free will given by God, so as He freely gives and we receive, we freely give Him our hearts, and He receives us back to Him. That is love, and freedom is love. Free will used for oneself is how sin entered the world, and so death came. Free will is only the intended blessing when it is for God. He is the only good source of anything. People make choices all of the time, and they are not always for good. Sin is death and nothing else, just the end of good. God is truth and perfect and cannot dwell among sin. Sin had to be dealt with so we could have a relationship with God again. God gave us freedom over our choices and chooses to not control us. An example of this is when God first spoke to Samuel. "The LORD came and stood there, calling as at the other times, 'Samuel! Samuel!' Then Samuel said, 'Speak for your servant is listening'" (1 Samuel 3:10). Samuel had to welcome God to speak to him. He uses His sovereignty for love, not control. God is the Creator and the only source of good. He uses His sovereignty to bring life, not control, and does not take away good things. We do that ourselves if we are not focused on Jesus and our spirits.

Many are afraid of God. I was taught to be afraid that if I failed, He would strike me down. The Israelites never denied God's power. They just did not see it for good and that it was all for love. They did not see His love for them. The Israelites were motivated by fear.

God is motivated by love only. Our choices not only affect ourselves but others as well. This is just another reason why we need to choose for Him to guide our lives through the Holy Spirit. We will always be where we should be and at the right place at the right time. If we fail to listen, this is when He will always turn bad things around for good. He does not cause bad things. I have heard in many places, like in church, music, and many other places, that God is in control. Jesus says we have authority provided by Him. We are not to live as if we are just hanging on to hope if God wants good for us. He already created everything and sent Jesus to provide everything we would need to be saved and redeemed. We are to walk boldly for Christ. One thing that God has made clear is that He will choose when the end of this sinful world will come and when the new heaven and earth will be. He is the only one who knows when Jesus will come back, not even Jesus. He is not secretive but honest and protective, a Father and a Friend always. This is why we should not wait to choose to be saved and receive the baptism of the Holy Spirit. God is telling us that by not saying when the end will come and the new beginning start. This is grace and mercy.

There is a godly anger; He does not like sin because sin is death. He is life and perfection. In His Word (Deuteronomy 28), He reveals to us the blessings and the curses that are brought for not staying true to Him because He is everything good. He wants blessing, not cursing. If we did not have a choice, He would not provide information. He made the way for Jesus in all that He was doing after sin entered the world. One thousand years is like one day to God. All this has just been pointing to Jesus, who is God in the flesh with a physical body. He is what grace is; He is love. Remember, grace is free, a gift of love and mercy. We do not receive due punishment because of mercy. Jesus took on all sins for us. God knew we could not do what Jesus could only do. Everything has pointed to Jesus since before His birth on this earth. Every time the Israelites had someone to lead them, they did not turn from God for a while. Once that person or his family died or they grew tired of that king, they went back to worshiping other false gods. They would worship things that they had to build that did nothing for them. The Israelites had to do everything. Jesus is the only way that is right and forever lasting. Jesus changes us forever. Death is behind the saved. The only death we see is to self, the old self. The only thing that is old is the old self when we are born again in Christ.

Jesus's finished work gave us the ability to use our free will for good and to have God's Spirit as close as close can be—within us to guide us until everything is made new and the world is no longer sinful. It is our spirit that becomes perfect like Jesus when we accept Him. Jesus brings our spirit back to life, perfect like God intended. Our souls and bodies must be renewed in this truth. When we are born again, we are freed from sin and all its effects. The world is not yet. We must walk with God and not the world. We are to walk in what we have so sin does not still affect us. The Holy Spirit is God's Spirit within us that guides us with that and helps us move in this fallen world. God is peace. He patiently did everything for us to be reconciled to Him and not just have Him beside us but within our hearts. God does not make mistakes. People do. God does not bring bad things. We do. He is the God of love, and Jesus is the Prince of Peace. Love and peace with God then and only then leads to love and peace among men for those who believe. When we become born again and have a brand-new just like Jesus's spirit, this is when we must spend the rest of our time on earth renewing our minds (souls and physical bodies) to what we have in our perfect righteous spirit thanks to Jesus and trusting in Him. Then, we need to share this. Our righteous spirit is our true identity and who we were created to be. Our soul is not all we are; it is our feelings and personality. Our flesh (physical body) is the house of our soul, but life is only in our born-again spirit. Houses do not have life; the people that live in them bring life into the house. A house on its own will just be quiet and empty. Our spirit is our true identity, not our physical body. We access our spirit by faith.

We must be born again because we were born into a corrupted, sin-filled world. Our spirit is not alive and righteous until Jesus. When we realize we cannot do and that, we can only do with Christ, praise God, we have found life. God is to get the glory; if He does, you know you are doing the right thing. He turns one into one thousand. He takes three hundred to ten thousand. He will forever provide abundance in all things. He will also use very little with the right motivation. He will not use anything without heart. His blessings and gifts are abundant. However, He does not require using big things. He just requires an open heart for Him.

God always corrects those that He loves and covers us, too, in the process. We always have grace and mercy. However, we still have flesh in this fallen world. Remember, bad news travels faster than ever with the misuse of technology. People are even inclined to spread lies just to get the attention they can get because now everyone has an opportunity to be heard all over the world right from their own homes. There is plenty of opportunity for pride. Imagine what could happen if we used technology and our voices for good—God's glory. Instead, God gets blamed for everything. When asked why God allows this or why bad things happen, the answer is usually, "I don't know." The reason for that is because He did not cause it or do it. He will use it out of His abounding grace and mercy to turn things around for good. God always brings something good out of the bad things I encounter every time. Knowing this truth sets you free. We must live in this world from the inside out or we keep believing lies or going back to lies. How many times do you hear someone actually saying the truth, and the truth is blaming the devil for the bad in this world?

Even believers say, "God did this once in the Old Testament; He will do it again." That is wrong! That cannot be; it is called "the Old."

The Old Testament was based on the law that brought death. We are in the new covenant of grace, the New Testament, that brings life. God has only ever wanted good for us. It is sin that brought punishment and required atonement. It is finished and was finished over 2,000 years ago when Jesus endured what we could never handle or even imagine. He also suffered on the cross completely alone. If we just meditate on that, there would be a whole lot more humility. I have thought it almost unbearable when I have had a family issue, and I am crying in the safety of my own home. Just think about this for even a minute: Jesus had everyone leave Him. He was completely separated from God. Thinking about that will change our attitude overall and toward any problem we may face. We are always victorious. We must walk in the victory. It starts with faith, not by what we see with our physical eyes.

Life by our own standards always leads to destruction. How can we have good if we do not include the source of good, which is God? When we surrender ourselves to Christ and submit our free will to Him, we will always rise. God will always raise us up at the appointed time (when we are ready). We must be born again for this to happen. He must be within us. If we do not have the source, there is no way to receive the blessing. It is like a plant with no water; it will not work. God's Word (the Bible) is the water that cleanses us. It is the only mirror we should consider important and see ourselves through. The Bible is our spiritual mirror. The Bible is for us not to read to please God. It is the instruction manual to live life inside out in this fallen world. His Word is like an indestructible bubble that encompasses us from this sinful world, just like Jesus gives us a new born-again spirit that cannot be touched by anything.

This world runs on a money system. Money is the motivation. Kingdom mindset is living according to God. He does not have a money system. Motivation in the kingdom mindset is faith in God and His love for us. His kingdom is based on love. Jesus said, "Give, and it will be given to you" (Luke 6:38). Since this world is money-motivated, we tend to think He was just speaking of money or possessions. He is God in the flesh. Money is not a God system. It is a system that God can work through with the free will of someone being an open vessel or usable for Him and His purpose since this world does run on money. However, Jesus did not have money on His mind. Why would He? His thoughts and motivations were set on God and will forever be. His focus was and is love forever. He was saying to love one another. We do this by opening our hearts and walking by faith. This is love.

We give to receive. We give Jesus our hearts to receive His perfect spirit, reunification with God, and eternal life with Him. The kingdom is love and starts with and functions on one action, given through faith. Jesus gave it all before we did anything. We receive the best gift. God gave His only Son so He could receive us back to Him. We must open our hearts and give our hearts to Him in order to receive by faith. This is where it all starts. Love is what the kingdom runs on. Jesus was not directly talking about money. He was talking about love. Yes, all things, even money, abound when the motivation is love and the action is to give. Jesus was first talking about our hearts. We cannot receive Him if we do not first give Him our hearts. Luke 6:37 refers to not judging or condemning others so you will not receive the same and to forgive others so you are forgiven. It is all about giving what you would like to receive. We are to share Jesus with others. Give so they can, too, receive. That is what He is saying here.

Jesus did not judge or condemn so that we would not be judged or condemned. On the cross, He said, "Forgive them, Father, because they know not what they do" (Luke 23:34). His purpose was so we could be forgiven and live loved. Everything has spiritual symbolism that we will see if we live by the spirit. The next verse in Luke 23:34 goes on to say how those watching him on the cross divided His garments and cast lots for them. He was doing this for all to be forgiven because we know not what we do. Until we receive Him, our spiritual eyes are closed, and we cannot see Him. This is why we are forgiven even before we sin. We can never see Him until we receive Him because we cannot see who He is until we receive a brand-new born-again spirit within us. Those watching Him on the cross could not see Him. God still used them and turned their evil around for good to show us Jesus is for everyone. The people divided His garments, showing us that Jesus is to be shared and is for us all. They had no idea. However, God did. He turned their bad actions around for good.

Jesus gave us forgiveness of sin, redemption from sin, and eternal life so we could receive and live abundantly. Sin can no longer bring death to the saved. God has the saved back, and we have reunification with God. We will not be judged or condemned. We are forgiven. We receive everything Jesus provided. As He sits at the right hand of the Father, so are we in this world (1 John 4:17). Jesus is not broken, sad, sick, or scared. He is strong, joyful, healthy, and strong. Remember, Jesus finished it and is waiting for us. He sits and rests now. This is key; we should rest in Him as we live in this world. God's Spirit is now within the saved and available to all who are willing to be guided by Him. This is why Jesus said it was better that He go and not stay. He said we would have the Comforter (the Holy Spirit). This is because we now have God within us, hugging and protecting our born-again spirit. When Jesus walked this earth, He would walk alongside people. Now that He finished it, gave us a new spirit to receive, and went to the Father, we were given what God originally intended. On this earth, we receive His spirit inside of us, not just on the side of us. We are truly never ever alone again. Give, and you will receive, is the way of the kingdom.

I had to take on the responsibilities of adulthood at a young age. I was emancipated at sixteen and had to sign out of high school and get a GED so I could focus on working and getting a trade. I was told by the principal that I had to bring back all my books to each teacher one by one. I brought my history book back to my teacher at the time. She told me in front of everyone that I would not become anything. I just had this peace that I could not explain at the time. I just knew that was not true. Years later, I was blessed with knowing to forgive her because she knew not what she was doing. In her mind, she thought she was helping me because where she was was all she knew. God's plans are never for bad. No, He did not plan for those bumps in my life. God gives us free will. He does not control the choices those around us make either. Remember that. He will turn everything around for good every time.

God's plans are also not the world's either. I think of Mary and how she had to trust God as people talked about her, not understanding she was carrying the Messiah. I also think of Noah building an ark when there had not been any rain, and all the people talked about him and laughed at him. There are many Bible accounts such as these. We are to live by faith, and remember they know not what they do. Have mercy and spread Jesus. It has got to be about God, not the opinions of people who are always empty and mean nothing in the kingdom of God.

I will go back to when I was in school. It was in ninth grade when it first appeared to me that writing was something that I did not know I had the ability to do. I had struggled in English before that time. Suddenly, I was writing and did not know where it came from at the time. I went to college at the age of twenty-six and even skipped English classes because my professors submitted my work with the request I needed to move to the next level. That is God. At the time, I did not know why this was happening. He works in beautiful ways. I have put this ability to use many times before to try and help others in different ways. Now, it was time for this book. It is so clear that we must know who He is, and that starts with reading

His Word. However, first, we need to know that we have a spirit, not just a soul. The two are not the same.

We are to read the Bible from our spirit. God is a spirit who made us in His image and spirit that was then corrupted by the fall of Adam. God gave us Jesus to provide redemption that brought a perfect born-again spirit just like Jesus's spirit, ready and waiting for any who will believe with their whole hearts. In this book, I pray you will understand the importance of even knowing you have a spirit. God is a spirit, Jesus makes your spirit perfect and righteous (right with God), God's Word is spirit breathed by Him, and we read His Word by our spirit, not our logic. It is by faith, not logic. God is bigger than logic. I also hope you receive Jesus and all that He provided for all of us—every single one of us. I talk to so many people who do not know this. I once did not and suffered greatly. I pray to be usable and a vessel for God. I hope I am one of many He is invited to work through so He can be known to all as the Perfect Father and Friend that He is and always has been.

Remember, the Bible is to be read by the spirit, not the brain. God is above logic. He is the voice of reason. He is the author of good and the answer to everything. There will be fruit from His Word. Promise! God's Word, the Bible, is God-breathed. There are no mistakes. The writers did not misinterpret. They were led by the Holy Spirit to write exactly what God said. When "LORD" is in all capital letters, this is referring to God. When "Lord" has just one capital letter, this is referring to Jesus as Lord. We also must remember that the Bible is not always or just referring to an abundance of money and food. Those are examples and fruit from His Word. Remember, God's kingdom is above a system and is not based on either money or food. It runs on God and His love. He is grace. His Word is always referring to give, and you will receive, seek and you will find because this is how the kingdom works.

Do it willingly (seek) with your free will to receive what God gave to us so we can receive life with Him. We are made in His image

(Spirit) to take that path. Then, when sin entered the world, He made the way to give us our Savior, Jesus, so that we could receive eternal life and all the blessings with it again. In turn, we go and share Jesus with the world so others can receive. This is the kingdom mindset. God will provide all things and work through people who are willing. He will always make a way where there seems to be no way (Isaiah 43:16). Money comes in as a factor because the world runs on a money system. God does not have money; the world has currency. He does not take what is not for Him. God works through people with money and anything else we need to live and move in this world to spread His Word. Jesus is the life-giving water and the bread of life. Whoever comes to Him will not go hungry or thirsty (John 6:35). Even the food we eat and the water we drink are symbolic and point to Jesus and that we need Him to have life. Again, God does not cause bad things. The Bible clearly shows over and over He has always been trying to save and protect.

We have free will. This is why God does not stop everything. He cannot because then His Word would be a lie; He would be dishonest. Everything would collapse because everything stands on His Word, the one and only truth and source of good. When sin entered the world through Adam, death came. People became evil in their hearts because their spirits were no longer connected to God, good, or lived by anymore. Everyone in this world is born with a corrupted spirit. This is why everyone must be born again through Jesus. After the fall, people started living first by their flesh because their spiritual eyes were closed. This is how Adam and Eve became aware that they did not have clothes on. They became aware of their flesh and were living first from their flesh. People and their choices cause bad things to happen. God is not willing for any to hunger, be thirsty, or ever be hurt. God is everything good, and sin is everything bad. There is no in-between.

God cares about your heart, your motive, and not how perfect you do something. If someone is offended, they are convicted, and that is the first step, so praise God. Two different things will happen when we share Christ, either someone is joyful to receive or first offended. If you get neither, you do not share your heart. You held back. Fear has to do with punishment. There is no fear with God because, through Christ, we are made perfect, righteous (right with God), and completely loved. It is the greatest freedom we will ever know to come to the end of ourselves and truly rely on God. Praise God! He has always tried to love and protect His people. He spoke through prophets, directly to Moses even. Jesus came and was God in the flesh, and now we have the Holy Spirit within anyone who has Jesus in their heart. Just please remember, the Holy Spirit will not be able to lead and guide you until you, by free will, choose to welcome Him to do so. This is something many of us are not told and, therefore, why we have so many converts instead of disciples producing spiritual fruit. People are just saved and stuck settling for what is, and the devil is having a party.

Jesus Himself received the baptism of the Holy Spirit before He went into the desert and was tempted by the devil for forty days (Luke 4:1). The focus was not water baptism. He did not need a washing away of sin; He is sinless. Jesus is the living water who makes us clean. This is what He was showing us when He was baptized in the water by John the Baptist. He received the baptism of the Holy Spirit first, and then He called us to be baptized with the same. We must choose Him, and then we can receive what He did, which brings the gift of the Holy Spirit—God's Spirit within us. He did it, and we get to receive it. Praise God!

Remember, even the devil knows that God exists. The enemy also knows Scripture, which he spoke to Jesus about while tempting Him for forty days in the wilderness. The wilderness represents how the devil tries to manipulate us by our choice. He tries to get us alone or to get us to think we are alone and, therefore, weak instead of strong in Christ. The enemy recognizes that God exists and His Word exists.

However, the enemy just twists it and questions it. The enemy uses the Old Testament against us and works on what we do not know. We have to read with our spirits and our hearts to see. The enemy tries to work on our minds (physical bodies). He has no power. He can only do this if we give permission. The saved have a new spirit that cannot be touched.

Remember, God corrects whom He loves. The priest Eli had two sons who were dishonest. Eli did not correct them. He knew what they were doing but did nothing about it. He put his sons above God, and he suffered because of it. Disobedience and honoring others before God is sin, and sin brings death and destruction. If Eli had corrected his sons, he would have honored God and shown true love to his sons, also. Instead, Eli and both of his sons suffered needlessly. The whole point is that none of them could do what was right without the saving grace of Jesus. We would do the same thing and put our children or others before God if not for what Jesus did. He redeemed us and did what we could not do. Jesus showed us what love really is. It is spiritual, not physical. He saves us and changes us in a way we could never change on our own. We give to receive. We are to give our heart and trust in Jesus, not ourselves, just as God first gave to receive us back to Him. We are not to try to be someone's god or someone else be ours. We have one true God who is and who loves us.

In the Old Testament, Samuel addressed Israel because they rejected the true king, God. They wanted a person to lead them so that they could see with their physical eyes and be like other countries they had seen. They went by outward appearance as well. They wanted what only Jesus could give us all. He is the only one to willingly shed His blood for His people to have the kingdom. He chose us before we chose Him because He loves us. Choosing a king is putting a person before God. A person in this fallen world chosen as king could not work because the king himself was sinful. The same is true today with government leaders; they cannot lead the people in good if they themselves do not first have Jesus and the truth that comes with Him as well. Samuel anointed Saul as king. Saul did not walk in faith and wait and trust that God would always come through. He tried to help God out at times. It never worked, and he fell. Samuel disapproved of Saul and told him what he would face because of his lack of faith and poor choices. "But now your kingdom will not endure; the LORD has sought out a man after his own heart and appointed him ruler of his people, because you have not kept the LORD's command" (1 Samuel 13:14). One cannot lead anyone who is not saved by Jesus and without the voice of reason that is only found in God. He was always supposed to be our king.

God rejected Saul, and he was then tormented by an evil spirit. Life becomes death without God. Saul needed God and should not have tried to be like God. He destroyed his own life, not God. Saul ended up going to see a medium to try to consult Samuel, who had died because he was cut off from God and was afraid of what would happen to him. Communicating with mediums or anything like that and not seeking God is wrong. Mediums, psychics, tarot card readers, or anything like that are not of God. We do not consult the dead or anything other than God to receive information about the living. The Bible tells us so; the Bible is the instruction manual. Without it, it is going to be a mess. It is just like trying to put something together without reading the instructions; it will not work. One tiny piece could be missed and ruin the whole thing. Every piece is important.

"Do not turn to mediums or seek out spiritists, for you will be defiled by them. I am the LORD your God" (Leviticus 19:31). We cannot seek light in dark places. He is not in dark places. "Consult God's instruction and the testimony of warning. If anyone does not speak according to this word, they have no light of dawn" (Isaiah 8:20). I was once asked to go see a psychic and also see someone who read tarot cards. I did think about it because I did not know better. I was feeling empty and longing for direction. This was before I knew who Jesus was and what I already had in Him. Not knowing better is just as wrong and damaging as knowing and making a poor choice. We can all see the state of the world because His Word needs to be shared. I then had this pull to turn from that, and praise God I did. Remember, I was saved at ten years old. I had everything I could ever need. I just did not know that yet.

Now that I look back at the decision to not go to a psychic, which was about twenty years ago, I know why I turned from that. It was the Lord's protection, the new nature I had been given in my spirit. Even if you did do something like this, you are already forgiven. Sin has been dealt with on the cross. When you get saved, your nature in your spirit is changed to life and righteousness from death and darkness. Let Him guide you, and you will turn from sin. It is an absolute. It is grace, and true God-given grace always brings us away from sin. Your forgiveness was already provided through the cross. Receive that and the blessings that come with it.

Guilt is a result of sin. Guilt is used by the enemy and the flesh in this world. Rest in forgiveness. Reside there. Whether you are learning, sharing, and/or receiving, if God gets the glory, then it is right. Come expecting. That is faith. It is like a woman knowing she is expecting a baby. She is expecting she will receive a baby in her arms and see it with her eyes. It is so exciting. The kingdom mindset is to set your focus on God, be excited, and expect greatness. Just as we do not deny a baby is coming, we are not to deny the love of God and what Jesus has already done.

David was a man after God's own heart; that is why God raised him up as king after Saul. David did not have what we now do, a brand-new born-again spirit or the Holy Spirit within him. He had to "go" and consult God. One account of this is in 1 Samuel 30:7–8: by putting on an ephod, which is a sleeveless garment worn by Jewish priests, David went and consulted God. That is what he had at this time. David used it and inquired of God, not anyone else. We have so much more now. We have the opportunity to receive Jesus's spirit and be born again and to connect to God and His Spirit, the Holy Spirit within us, to lead us. We do not have to go and seek any longer; He is right there. We have Him as close as can be. With that being said, let us remember not to pray as David did. He did not have what we have. We are to pray in thankfulness and praise, not begging and pleading. David wrote many wonderful psalms. They bless us or they would not be in the Bible. We just must remember to view them as they were, the *Old* Testament that was pointing to Jesus all along. We have what even David did not have at that time. We have complete redemption with God right now.

Just knowing God exists is not the way to eternal life. We must accept Jesus, who brings the finished work of the cross to be saved from eternal condemnation, receive eternal life, and have a relationship with God. Jesus is the door, not you or any kind of religious practice or tradition, even if it is about God Himself. He gave us free will because He is love. We must submit our lives to Christ and to His will for our lives so that we do not miss the awesome things He has for us. We just need to reach out and take. It is godly to come boldly to the throne and take what is yours. God loves that because that is faith. There is godly boldness, just like there is godly anger. This is the one good kind of anger, and all that means is to not like sin, to turn away from it. God is peace, not war. I often wondered why we had anger as an emotion. Then, it was revealed to me that it was given with godly purpose as protection from sin. In this world, boldness can be called bullying, and taking can be called greed if it is not for God. With godly purpose, boldness is faith and taking what is yours, receiving is love to God. Please catch this. God does not want us to hide; He wants to see our faces and live in relationship forever.

A baby being baptized is not receiving Christ. This is just a religious ceremonial action that does not reach God and does not provide salvation through Jesus. Receiving Jesus is an individual independent choice to make and relationship to have. He is the only Savior, the only source of salvation, which is deliverance from sin and death. "If you declare with your mouth, 'Jesus is Lord,' and believe in your heart that God raised him from the dead, you will be saved" (Romans 10:9). It starts with just me and Jesus. Babies do not have that ability. They cannot believe with all their heart because they are not even aware of their feelings or how to use them yet. We believe by faith and choose from our souls to receive what Jesus did to save us and receive our perfect born-again spirit by faith. Our perfect born-again spirit and our soul make up our whole hearts. This is how we believe with all our hearts. Jesus was born as a baby, too, and had to grow and learn who he was in the Father. God will not hold babies accountable either because they have not reached a point of being responsible for their choices.

The Bible does not name a specific age because that is not how God measures. He measures from the motivation of our hearts. Everyone has their own journey and purpose. He would not give one specific age because that is not just and changes amongst different individuals in this fallen world. We all have different circumstances. Just as sin was not imputed until the law was given and responsibility for choices was then placed, children who have passed go to heaven because God is just, and He is love. He will not ask us to do something that we cannot do. "And the little ones that you said would be taken captive, your children who do not yet know good and bad—they will take possession of it" (Deuteronomy 1:39). The land Israel was to possess was on earth at that time. However, it was to be a walk of faith with God as the supplier of everything. They were just asked to walk in obedience, which is faith also. The land they were to possess was both symbolic and a revelation of God's kingdom being restored with the new heaven and the new earth. I pray you see that just as I have because He revealed this to me in His Word. It was not just about land. It is about God's kingdom. God says so, and so for us to be able to enter the kingdom, we must do so like a little child, humbling ourselves. "See that you do not despise one of these little ones. For I tell you that their angels in heaven always see the face of my Father in heaven" (Matthew 18:10). God would never place anything on us that we could not do. This is why He sent Jesus.

See Yourself as He Sees You

Knowing who God is gives us our one true identity of who we are, which is only found in Christ. We need to see ourselves as He sees us in Christ. Just think of white, fluffy clouds in the sky on a sunny day. This brings a joyful feeling. That is how God sees His people. God sees us through Jesus. He sees us as pure and perfect in our born-again spirit. God does not see us through our physical bodies. He sees us from the inside at our deepest point, our spirit that is just like His Son. Jesus provided everything good for us and defeated everything that sin brought, which is, first, death. God is young forever, and so are we. Bring Him in everything. Jesus is the door; God is the union. If you ask anyone what is important to them, they are likely to say they need to know their purpose. Can I tell you? Simply, after many hard years and many mistakes later, our purpose is to first be loved by God. That is the root, and from there, the fruit on the vines will grow and flow like a stream. Every good thing and fulfillment of all kinds comes from His love, just being loved by Him. That was something I never heard until about six years ago. However, I did not have "ears to hear." My heart was hardened to this "works" mentality. Now I know that I need to be a branch that shares but how God wants me to share not how I think I should. God does not need my help. He needs me to be usable and not about myself because if I am, then the blessing becomes a curse. He needs my heart to simply be open for Him and nothing else.

As His Word says, pride always goes before a fall. You will know when it is God when you realize the things you know you should do require Him to be with you. I could not write a book on my own. By worldly standards, I am completely unqualified. I am someone who has fit many statistics that should have fallen. But Jesus saved me. I was on my own at a very young age, did not finish high school, have been in many bad places and situations, somehow went to college and did well, and well, just by His grace, I am here to tell you about all of it.

At the age of twenty-seven, I got married, and my son was born a couple of years later. Not long after that, we moved to a different state, which meant I could not continue at the college I was attending. I was going for nursing only because I was brought up to think I was somebody if I earned a college degree and went into the medical field. It was not my calling at all. I always knew that. We do not go by circumstances, even if they are favorable. Before I ever went to college in the first place, I had received a scholarship to pay for all of my tuition. I greatly appreciated that beyond words, but I still knew in my heart this was not what I was supposed to be doing. I did do well, and after we moved and my daughter was born, I got back to it, but again, for the wrong reasons. I had reached the point for clinicals and had just been fitted for my clinical uniforms. All I had to do was show up to start clinicals. As I walked out into the parking lot that day after finishing every step needed to start learning in a hospital, God spoke. I literally stopped and said, "Okay." He said no. I listened, and I am forever thankful that I did. I had done everything in college based on longing for acceptance from my family. This was my motivation for going there in the first place. I did not enjoy any part of it. When something went well, my first thought was always that maybe my family would be proud. That is wrong. We are not to earn love and acceptance. This only comes from Jesus first, and it is not earned.

Because we are not taught about grace as we should, what seems to happen and with so many bad things at our fingertips on a touch screen is people going deeper into sin instead of away. I hear so many speaking from a low standpoint, "Oh, just an old sinner saved by grace." Wrong. When you are saved, you are the righteousness of God in Christ, wonderfully brand-new and young forever because of the free, forever gift of grace that is provided only through Jesus. We are new and right with God; that is what righteousness means, now right with God. When He sees you as a believer, He only sees what Jesus did, not what you do. Please remember, God is a spirit, Jesus is God with a body, and the Holy Spirit is the Teacher provided to be within us as close as close can get to comfort and guide us in this fallen world.

We are in the world, not of it. Do not live in the Old Testament, which was to show us we needed Jesus the whole time. In both the Old Testament and New Testament, we are shown God's forever love, grace, and mercy to His people. However, we are to live in the new. People make bad choices, not God. He cannot dwell amongst sin because He is perfect! The Israelites waiting forty years in the wilderness was not for punishment but by grace because they were not ready to possess the land God had for them. God wants to always bless us, not curse us. This time, the wait is for us, so we are ready to receive the blessing. Now we have Jesus and can receive the blessing and live in it forever. We all fall short without Him. God is resting and waiting patiently for all to have a chance at eternal life. When we know the truth, as when the law was given sin began to be imputed, we have a responsibility to share the truth. That is not work but rest in love. This is where freedom comes from. What you do know will save you, and what you do not know will destroy you. We all must decide to stop following people and follow Jesus.

Even Christmas has become a profit-making time. Remember the temple? Jesus told the Pharisees that they had made God's temple a den of thieves. Think about the burden and debt many of us have been in to get gifts instead of being blessed and sharing the blessing. December 25th is not even Jesus's actual birthday. Remember, calendars change. God does not. Jesus's finished work does not expire. Jesus said that people have let go of God's commands to hold on to human traditions (Mark 7:8). This is talking about anything religious, ceremonial, or repeated acts of so-called worship and traditions like celebrating His birth. It is not about any of these things. It is about walking in the gift we were given only by Jesus. It is about living in a posture of thanksgiving, not circumstances. Here is a big news flash: we all have free will. There will not only be good favoring circumstances. If you do not reside in circumstances, they cannot touch you. Believers live in the world and are of the finished work of Christ. Unbelievers or those who have not accepted salvation through Jesus are of the world and live moment to moment—good or bad. How it goes is how they live. The true meaning of Christmas is to stay in thanksgiving and remembrance. Jesus's birth was the greatest new beginning miracle ever that led to what miraculous things we have now only in Christ.

The devil does not always have to work hard or appear scary. Look, Christmas has become represented by a man in a red suit. How odd is that? And that is the enemy at work. He totally twists things to the opposite of what they should be. It can appear so subtle and even attractive and fun. Death does not just come in a scary form; it can be masked by a nice exterior. Hint: why we do not go by the outside of things or physical appearance in people. Just the whole gift-giving thing is an absolute lie from the get-go. We are making it again about us and our works. To love someone is to tell them the only true gift you will ever be given that will last and not perish is Jesus. Giving someone a gift should not be the focus. It is a nice gesture that, in the right place, will bring a smile to someone, and that is, of course, a beautiful thing, but in its place. Think about it: the gift list, even for adults, starts again maybe a week later or before Christmas. We always have a wish list because those things do not last, and that is what the devil wants us to focus on.

Remember, the enemy does not always come in scary form. Suttle, sneaky, and dishonesty are his main tactics. Jesus said in Matthew 15:3 that we disobey God to follow man and tradition. Even the holiday celebrated can become someone's god if that is where their heart is; it is about Jesus, not the tradition itself. We should live in appreciation and awareness of Him every day. We do not even have the exact date for Christmas or Easter. The Bible does not say because that is not what is important. If the Bible does not tell us, it is not what we should be focused on. Easter has become about a bunny and eggs instead of when Jesus set us all free.

Cling to Jesus, not a Christmas tree. We should sing to God, not the tree. There is nothing wrong with a tree if it is not the source. It can be a beautiful symbol that must point to Jesus to be good. It is like a koala that clings to a tree. It is so strong and holding on well but at such peace. It is not the tree that makes this possible. The tree is just the thing it is grabbing. Its ability to hold on comes from the way God designed it. The baptism of the Holy Spirit (the Teacher, the Comforter) gives us all we will ever need on this earth to live in the fullness of Christ now, not later. Jesus gave us the great commission when all authority over heaven and earth was given to Him. He said to go and share and bring others to what was now available. We must first see ourselves in His promises. Psalm 103:5 says He satisfies our desires with good so that our youth is renewed like the eagle's. We are made new not to grow old but to prosper. See the vast good things that He has for you, the fun. He gets all the glory then, and only then is when you are free and can enjoy and rest. So, rest.

Who we are is not the shell we have on the outside. We make our body our god and put all our attention yet again to ourselves and focus on the part that is the farthest point of us away from God. We then wonder why He feels so far away, and we just feel empty and longing to be filled. Again, God is a spirit, not flesh. When I was a teenager and until I was in my thirties, I would not go anywhere without makeup. I would not even go put gas in my car without makeup. This had become like a god or idol to me. It defined my life. I had to do that before I would leave the house or go outside. The issue is if we do not have our identity in Christ, something is going to get our attention and become a vice, as makeup was once for me. I did not see myself as God sees me. Instead, we need to use mirrors for good purposes, not to look for what is wrong. Let us make an effort to see what is right with us in a mirror, not what is wrong. God makes wonderful things, not flawed. It starts by first seeing yourself in your true identity that can only be seen in the spiritual mirror that is God's Word. Anything can become an idol. In modern times, it can be the phone. If something rules your day or is always the deciding factor in your life, and it is not God, it is an idol.

Remember, God made us all intelligent. Everyone is given the ability to take in information and use it in some way. We all have access to wisdom through Jesus Christ and the Holy Spirit. We are guided away from sin and to make good decisions. We are given information and experience that we did not have to walk through to get as Jesus did and freely shared with any who would receive it. "For God does not show favoritism" (Romans 2:11). He did not make anyone more special than another or give to one and not the other. Anything that is not good is not God. It is sin and the evil one. Jesus saves us from this, redeems us, heals us, and makes us brand-new. This world uses the word smart. Someone is smart if they are quick with something because the world has one speed: fast. Intelligence is what matters and is given to all. God made no two people alike with good purpose and does not favor one above the other. Even if two people are said to be identical twins, science only takes us so far. There will be something that determines who is who because that is God. We were made to be one with God, not just like another person. There is no limit to God. The only part of us that is made to be identical is we all receive the same spirit from Jesus, so we are saved. God made us in His own image in spirit. Jesus reunites us with God because we receive a new spirit, Jesus spirit within us, full of life and love. "Now to each one the manifestation of the Spirit is given for the common good" (1 Corinthians 12:7). Everything is made for the good of all, not just one, and God always gets the glory. That is how we are blessed because He gives so we can receive. To love Him is to receive what He has given. He is fair; He created everything that way. We are made to live as one body of Christ. We all cannot be the head or the foot. The body would not work. "Just as a body, though one, has many parts, but all its many parts form one body, so it is with Christ" (1 Corinthians 12:12). So, just because someone may approach something differently does not mean it is wrong or that something is wrong with them. Everything does not have to be quick to be right. It is about what you are trying to do, where you are trying to go, and getting there. It is not about how one started; all that matters is how you finish. We should measure everything to God's kingdom; what matters is that we see it, not how quickly we get there or how we started. We want to end up there and not perish. The finish line is more important than the start line. The start has potential for good; the finish is the end of a road. It is the end of a choice. There is either life eternal or death and condemnation forever. Our true beginning does not start until we accept Jesus in our lives. Before that it is merely existence and falling slowly. We should first measure anything to God's Word, His written instructions, which is the Bible. If it goes against His Word, there is no question it is wrong. If it aligns with His Word, it is right. That is it, clear as can be. There is right and wrong and good and bad. There is no in-between.

My family and I tried to find a church and just could not find one at the time that was just about Jesus and taught about what all His finished work provided for believers. We started watching Andrew Wommack and Joseph Prince online, and this completely changed our lives. We started hearing the truth about God's grace. It is all about grace. I would choose to gather as a God-defined church under a metal roof in the heat, struggling to hear from the rain hitting the roof and hear the truth of His Word any day. Then and only then can we connect as the body of Christ. It cannot be about a fancy building. Then, the church is disconnected, lost, and confused. The beauty is even if I could not hear from rain hitting a metal roof with my physical ears, my spirit hears the Word of God. If the truth is preached, the truth is always received. It is just up to us to use it. We must choose God's path. If someone is led to start a big church or go to one, and that is led by God, it is right and just. If it is God's will for someone, God will use it. Just remember, we never need to help God out. We need to be usable, an open vessel for Him only.

I was brought up in a religion, really in name or label only, as my family did not consistently attend church or ever read the Bible. I had been baptized in a Catholic church as a baby at about three weeks old. About four years ago, I even tried to get water baptized, and just my paper got lost in the stack and somehow was found underneath a bunch of things. I was then told that water baptisms would not be done anytime soon because of something else going on with the church. At the time, I felt disappointed and lost. As you will hear me say in this book, we cannot go by what we feel. We have to go by what we know. Not long after that I received revelation knowledge about what I already had all along and just did not know.

What I had was Jesus since I was ten years old, and the baptism I was looking for was the Holy Spirit, which I received not long after trying to get baptized by water in front of everyone in the church as an adult. I have gently learned to live by God's calendar, not my own. Think about it: calendars change. The United States calendar changes, and there are many other forms of calendars that are all different. Man-made or worldly things change. God and His Word do not. Proverbs 21:21 spoke to me. "Whoever pursues righteousness and love finds life, prosperity, and honor." This is the verse I read when I knew I would write this.

When I was still in "a works mentality," I thought I needed to use all the time I could volunteering. I chose to go to this one place where I had to be interviewed to make sure I would be a good fit, as the subject matter carried a great deal of influence and responsibility. The lady I met with said I have a verse for you. A still, small voice. This is from 1 Kings 19:12–13, which says, "After the earthquake came a fire, but the LORD was not in the fire. And after the fire came a gentle whisper. When Elijah heard it, he pulled his cloak over his face and went out and stood at the mouth of the cave. Then a voice said to him, '"What are you doing here, Elijah?"' Exactly, what was I doing there? I was not there knowing who God really is, and I thought I had to earn His love and approval. Of course, we need to help others. However, it needs to be first knowing we are loved by Him and that we are just trying to share that love. We cannot share love if we are not first loved and know it. Andrew Wommack taught me that God cares about your motivation, not your action. There have always been bad things going on since the fall of man when Adam sinned. Notice the mercy of God that it was Adam's sin that changed everything. He was the first man and had firsthand information where Eve did not. She could be more easily deceived. We all can when we do not have truth. One issue today is technology is everywhere making communication so easy. Now, bad news travels fast. Think about what we have in front of us on screens, mostly bad news, not good news and truth. Bad news has been there but took more time and effort to spread in the past. Today, that is not the case.

It is important to know what grace really means. It is a free gift from God that is unearned by you and has nothing to do with your efforts. Mercy is not receiving due punishment for wrong choices and actions. The Bible has the words behold and beware used often. We should take a hint there. Behold means to focus and receive. Beware means to watch carefully. So, let me ask: do we not all just want to be loved, wanted, and accepted? It is something we all long for deeply, if we are honest. The only answer and supplier of these things is Jesus.

Personally, like many others, I have learned this the hard way. My prayer is for that to not keep happening to others. It does not have to because it is finished. This can happen in everyone's lives if and only if we know who God is and that Jesus's finished work on the cross is the provider of the things we long for most of all. We have to be able to see ourselves as He sees us. There is absolutely no other source of love; therefore, no other source of anything good. If God is not part of it, it cannot be good. Jesus is the only answer and solution. Live by grace, not traditions and ceremonies. Otherwise, we take our eyes off Jesus again and again. If we are honest, we have a longing, a need to be held because this is real and true. We are made to cling to Him, and that is good and life. It is not self, cling to Him. Clinging is only good when it is to the Lord. Let us not cling to religious ceremonies and traditions. This leads to emptiness and disappointment, waiting for the next Christmas, thinking that one might be better. True, right?

If we are not in God's Word, we take in lies or wrong information from one who misinterprets it quite a lot, even without knowing. Mark Chapter 6 plainly talks about the fact that Jesus had siblings. However, in love, I say I was brought up Catholic, and in my experience, it was a lot more about worshiping Mary than it is about anything about what Jesus did and provided. This is the opposite of what Jesus said to do. The devil tries to be sneaky and crafty, just trying to dilute and distract from what our Savior did for us. Mark 6 says how Jesus had siblings. Instead, we have those who believe Mary was a virgin for life who had no other children. However, Luke 2:7 refers to Mary giving birth to her firstborn son. It does not say only son, either. There is another account of when Jesus performed His first miracle and turned water into wine. "After this he went down to Capernaum with his mother and brothers and his disciples" (John 2:12). My personal walk with Catholicism was I was never encouraged to read the Bible myself; instead, I was told not to touch "the Book" by my parents. I was taught that it was untouchable. They were just doing what they were taught and knew how to do. I was brought to many funerals where a rosary was prayed. It felt so empty as it was ceremonial and not glorifying God. There was not the fruit of God's Word flowing anywhere around me in home, church, people, or anything. God's Word is true, is life, and will never return void. If one is in God's Word and not receiving secondhand information from someone else being dishonest or misinterpreting, they will flourish. The truth of His Word will produce fruit every time.

I was taught that we work our way through seven sacraments that are not mentioned in the Bible. This is not true and just creates a works mentality that we are just supposed to do this. Catch it and work through the seven sacraments. Jesus did all the work, not me. It does nothing for us but just seems like a checklist to meet. It is based on man instead of God and His never-failing life-giving Word. I remember feeling so empty, so far away, and that this was not right at all. People in the church were so cold unless they were family or friends. Even then, sometimes, it was just an empty situation.

We can only live by the spirit, not our flesh, in order to experience peace. Our flesh is division in this world. Everything is about looks in this world, and even some people base their worth or someone else's on the outside. This is not God. Our outermost part was not made for us to even focus on. It serves as a house for us. Hint: this is why we cannot just see ourselves without a mirror or picture. We should not be there. We should be living from the inside (our spirit), letting His beauty flow through to our souls and bodies, the outermost part. After sin entered the world, it divided us from God and one another. Our flesh (body) was intended to be a shelter, a system to serve us in our godly purpose, not to be lived by and dominated by at all. God is a spirit, not flesh. We have to live inside out so we do not have division. The evil one uses our flesh if we are willing to attack us from outside inward because he cannot reach us any other way.

Adam and Eve lived from the spirit. Because they first lived in a place without sin and with a perfect spirit, they had no awareness that they did not have clothes until sin entered the world and their spirit was cut off from God. Sin then brought death in all ways, shame, and condemnation. God is not willing that any should perish (2 Peter 3:9). Every person needs a savior who is only found in Jesus. "For we have all fallen short of the glory of God" (Romans 3:23). When you know that, wow, it is such a breath of fresh air. Rest. Remember, righteousness is being right with God—all sin being accounted for—atoned or atonement. We were created to live by our spirit. When sin happened, death was a result. This means death to the spirit, joy, love, and peace, not just physical death. We had to have an atonement to flip things back to what they should be. Now, because of Jesus, we have that choice. Remember, it is a choice because we are loved. It is not forced. If God does not force us to do things, we should remember not to blame Him for bad things or think He chooses to control everything. He is so loving and merciful. God left it up to us and waits for us.

The way now is to live inside out from the way the world lives. The world does everything according to the flesh (physical body and feelings), and this brings pride. The flesh in this current world is sinful and, therefore, filled with pride. Jesus made the way to live like we were intended to live—by our born-again spirit first and only. He made rivers flow with living water. This happens by living by our perfect born-again spirit, just like Jesus's spirit, and letting that run through to our souls and then bodies. Let Him hold you. God will make all crooked paths straight when we trust Him with our hearts. He has done this for me more times than I can remember. One time was when I knew I was supposed to homeschool my children. According to the world, I am not qualified. He says I am and that is what I am trusting. Let Him hold you like that. Cling to Him. We are taught to be independent and self-sufficient. There goes self again. This is teaching us a lie from the beginning. We were not created to do things alone. The true definition of independence is being free from outside distractions, not being led by them. We are to be led from the inside by the Holy Spirit guiding our spirit. In this fallen world, we do need rules to follow and have order. We need community with others. True independence is doing life with the Lord and clinging to Him not the opinions of people that change like the wind. When you live life with God, you will find love, joy, peace, strength, productivity, and rest. He is life. He is the source of life. Knowing this and living in it will bring us to the number of days He has set for us on this earth, not an alternative. There is no other right way. God set our number of days once. He is truth. He does not lie. Everything stands on His spoken Word of truth. He only sets good for us. He does not change it.

Doctors now tell people they are going to die on a regular basis. Not knowing, people take that in as doctrine and accept that fate. They make it their own, their identity. We cannot add one minute to our life. We can only take away time because we have free will. God is the only creator and giver of life. Live the number of days God has set for you. God created everything in six days, and when you came to be, He wrote the number of your days. God has given us free will out of love to choose. One thing He has kept is when Jesus will come back. We still have a choice to be ready and saved or not. Jesus does not even know the day. "Who of you by worrying can add a single hour to your life? Since you cannot do this very little thing, why do you worry about the rest" (Luke 12:25–26)? I am not saying do not see doctors; seek God, the Great Physician, first in all things in your life. He will never lead you wrong. Trust and rest. God is so merciful; He gave us doctors to help us since we did not have the truth to know Jesus healed us over 2,000 years ago. However, like anything without Him, it fell. Doctors used to serve the Lord and even make house calls. Now, you can barely see the doctor for a few minutes, if at all.

This has become a money-making venture instead of serving and caring for others. All we hear is about who is sick or what is out there. Signs along the road are mostly about illness, doctors, or awareness of something bad, not a real, everlasting solution. Awareness is good in the right context. The right context is God. Awareness of illness is fear. On its own, awareness is not a solution but instead leads to another problem. That is not from God. The truth is people are not purposely doing something negative. The issue is Jesus, in His fullness, is not shared so someone else can know and be set free. We must come to the end of ourselves and share His Word. Just as I believe and know I am saved, I must believe I am healed. They both come together. How can I think I am saved but not healed? That even defies basic logic. God wants us to be redeemed, healed, and prosperous. Jesus became poor so we could become rich in all ways! To trust Him is to claim God's Word over myself and others. If I say something is done, it is. It does not matter what someone thinks or if they question me. His Word never returns void, never! Living and resting in Jesus is putting an end to worshiping people and their opinions. It is a new beginning of serving others and loving them not based on their performance, as God loves me. His Word has to be all we need. It never fails. We do not go by what we see; we go by what we know. Let us look for the good and not just look for the bad.

 This may offend, but I have personally lived through the medical system of today and had to give it to God so I could go on. Because I did this, I could see how He turns things around for good always. I discovered that I was not supposed to be there or be sick. Cling to Him. He is divine health to you in all ways (spirit, soul, and body). This is your complete makeup. Again, our spirit is who we truly are, and as born-again believers, we are just like Christ in our spirit: perfect as God intended us to be and made in His image. Our soul is our personality and emotions. Our physical body is our "house," the outermost part of us that one day, along with our soul, will be perfect and complete, just like Jesus. I was not taught anything about being three parts or had ever heard anything about my spirit. I was told that the innermost part of me was my soul, and that is as deep as it went, or so I then thought. God is a spirit; we connect this way. We cannot connect if we do not know what we must begin with. His Word tells us what we have; we just must receive it by faith. He desires only our hearts. He receives that by our faith. He enjoys seeing us receive His blessings, which include love, joy, peace, health, and prosperity of all kinds. The key is using our prosperity for His purpose so that we and others may be blessed. I hear a lot of "this will move God." "Faith moves God." God has already moved. Our faith simply makes us aware of what is already there. It is like turning the light on in a dark room. The light is already available, but you must first flip the switch on. We act as if God is still punishing sin and that Jesus did not finish and provide everything. We act as if we ourselves still must add to what Jesus did. This is wrong. Our faith opens the door to receive what God already provided through Jesus over 2,000 years ago. The same is true of creation. God is not still creating. The Bible clearly states He created the earth in six days and then rested. He provided everything that would be needed on this earth. He said to be fruitful and multiply. It is up to us to use what God has already supplied. Then we bring forth "the fruit" that God already supplied that will not run out.

One morning, while taking some quiet time with the Lord I saw a vision in my heart (my spirit) of spreading my arms wide open and realizing why that is such a close to God feeling of peace. If we stand there with our arms wide open, we are making the image of the cross. Where did peace come from? It came from Jesus's finished work on the cross. When you discover who you really are, and that is only in Christ, comfort also comes in holding your arms close to you because He is within. Wow, what a blessing. To totally lose yourself and who you think you are is to truly live for the first time now and forever. Effort is not your works; it is to rest in Him forevermore. You know the term I hold dearly is whosoever. Wow, it is even stated "whoever" many times in the Bible. Jesus is for everyone, and God's Word points to that and that only good is with Him. Jesus does not have clicks, and God does not show favoritism. Everyone is welcome. Let us enter rest because it is finished. We are victorious already. Jesus sits at the right hand of the Father (God). He would not be sitting if the victory was not already provided. "Do not be afraid, little flock, for your Father has been pleased to give you the kingdom" (Luke 12:32). This verse is such a "fatherly hug." He wants to freely give to all of us. It is free, not based on what any of us do.

Praise God, when I was ten years old, I went to church with a friend. It was a Baptist church, and I remember being scared and kind of unsure because it was loud. I came from the Catholic church, which was repetitive and quiet. I was also taught that Catholicism is the one true religion. That never settled well with me. However, I did not know why at the time. Now, I know it was because it was not a true statement. Jesus is not religion at all because religion is man moving as if he is saved through his own works. We all need Jesus to not fail or live in evil. I remember the pastor asked people if they would come forward to accept Jesus. Honestly, I do not remember for some reason if I went up or stayed in my seat. I do know that I invited Jesus into my heart, and peace like I never knew was now there in that moment. Then, when my family did go to church, we went to the Catholic church, and the truth is I was saved and stuck. Praise God that I was now saved, though. I just speak over us all that God's people, the church, be truly based on Jesus and a church's financial or any needs be fully relied upon and entrusted to God to supply. Because the deal is He already has provided. We just have to reach out and receive by faith. He is not making anything else. He has already created everything we need during Creation. Anything that was needed after sin entered the world, Jesus provided and sealed when He died and rose again on the third day and went to the Father.

Obedience is better than sacrifice. All of the sacrifices that used to take place were an endless task because people just kept sinning. There could only ever be one perfect sacrifice, that is Jesus. Our Savior, Jesus Christ, put an end to all of the animal and other sacrifices and gave us true freedom and forever redemption. Obedience leads us to turn away from sin. Obedience in Christ always leads to more and more faith. The kingdom is not based on getting it right or someone else getting more right. Jesus is for everyone, not just certain people. It takes an open, ready-to-receive heart. That is all. It is not how you get there or how you start. It matters that you find Him and where you finish. Jesus got it all right for us all, so we do not have to because we could not ever. Through Him, we make the right choices.

Every good relationship and every good thing must start with the foundation of it is just me and Jesus first. I was watching a show one time where a guest who had just written a book shared a story that just profoundly stuck with me. It was about this lady who had been in prison, found Jesus, and was released from prison, living in the greatest and only true freedom of Jesus. This woman had started rapping in prison, saying, "It's just me and Jesus" the day she spoke her faith. I shared this story with my children, and now we smile and sing, "It's just me and Jesus." The beauty and blessings that happen when we share things like this change the world and touch people from any location. Just share! The enemy wants us to think, *It cannot be me; I am not good enough; God would not ask me, or I will just mess it up.*

Believers are meant to be missionaries. This world defines a missionary as someone who decides to live with little and go to foreign countries to share the gospel. A missionary is someone who is sent. Are we not all called to go and share? We are told in the Bible by Jesus telling the apostles to share the gospel with every creature (Mark 16:15). Therefore, a missionary is any believer. You can and are called to be a missionary. My daughter told me she wanted to be a missionary and go to hospitals and share Christ. I told her that she was a missionary and to just listen to the guidance of the Holy Spirit. Just as I once did, she, too, thought missionaries only go far away and only do certain things. I reminded her she is already a missionary and that it is not just for someone else who is willing to have little and go far away. The truth is, in the current state of things, there are many close by who do not know who Jesus is. There are plenty of believers who do not even know who God is, who Jesus is, and what He provided. Jesus also did not call anyone to be in poverty in any way. He became poor for us so that we may become rich. This is not just spiritual. Anything that is for God will prosper every time, whether spirit, soul, body, or something financially related. If the purpose is for the kingdom, and the motive is God, then it will happen every time.

My children and I read the book *These Are My People*. This is a book about the life of Gladys Aylward. She was a missionary to people in China. She endured so much and never quit. We were so inspired by her life. Personally, I was also inspired that much more to write this book because this woman did such wonderful things because of the Lord working through her. She was usable. However, I heard in the writing that she herself had not been told that Jesus healed all, and we have authority in Christ to speak healing over things and live in divine health. This woman walked her faith literally. She was even asked to calm a prison riot and did it. These men were listening to her like she was their mother. She walked in faith, and God never failed. "You shall eat the fruit of the labor of your hands: you shall be blessed, and it shall be well with you" (Psalm 128:2). Imagine the healings and even bigger changes that could have occurred in her journey had she shared all that Jesus provided. Andrew Wommack taught me something so important. Don't limit God by my small thinking. I am thankful to know Gladys's story and inspired to share Jesus.

All He needs is an open heart in faith. It is not about the opinions of others. It is about love for others. Jesus said, "As the Father loves me, so I also love you. Remain in love" (John 15:9). Jesus said we would do even greater works because we would have the Holy Spirit to guide all who accept Jesus and welcome Him to do so. We already have the victory that is not just for one person. We are to be joyful to spread the truth and hope greater the works will another do than I so all can be saved, not just some.

I hear so many people think they are supposed to experience sickness. *No!* Jesus took on every disease and conquered it. Just picture Him on the cross. It will get easier and easier to walk in. You must see it in your heart (your spirit) first. That is where the living water that is Jesus comes from. Through Jesus, God sees us as perfect, and that means healthy, too. Be careful for nothing (Philippians 4:6). Paul writes this, saying that we are not to worry about anything. Live in thanksgiving to God, and all is and will be well with you. We cannot go by what we feel; we have to go by what we know is true in God's Word. One cannot give what one does not know they have either. We must know we are loved and forgiven before we can love and forgive others and walk in health and strength. There is nothing we need to do to be forgiven. It was already done by Jesus, the greatest act of love. He did this before we were ever born to sin. It was done before we ever got started. Just believe in Him; that is it. Have faith in Him. It is not about you. Sin was dealt with over 2,000 years ago so we could have God again. God cannot dwell among sin because sin is evil. He loves you so much that He gave His only Son for you before you were born. Catch it, so you can have a choice to have Him and not have to fall first. The issue is we do not share this. That is why I am writing to you. Yes, you! I was watching Andrew Wommack one day, and he said the devil could not stop the resurrection, and he cannot stop your healing.

I am here to tell you that the devil is forever defeated. Healing of any kind is yours if you will receive it. The enemy (the devil) uses what we do not know against us. If we do not know we are already victorious, he will use that to try to get us to think we are defeated and should settle for sickness or anything bad hoping to recover and in our own power—not good at all. Wrong! By Jesus's wounds, we are healed (1 Peter 2:24). This is not just for when we get to heaven. There will not be a need to be healed in heaven because everything is perfect and free from sin in heaven.

Be saved and welcome the Holy Spirit and see. It will never return void, and there is no painful toil. The Lord is our king, not anyone else. Earthly kings are about self; look at the Old Testament. It is in there. We are not to worship wood or stone either. We are to worship God in spirit. Jesus saved you and gave us adoption into God's kingdom forever. It does not matter where you come from; catch that other thing pointing to the motive of our hearts, not our heritage or anything physical. It is all spiritual. Spirit is life; physical is death. The flesh (physical) is what the devil uses. God has always given and continues to give time to turn away from that. The things of this world will surely perish. His Word never will (Luke 21:33). You, in Jesus, will never pass away. Earthly kings have betrayed, and so have the people under them because everyone is longing for something more. We are all empty without God. Still today, without a king, the government all comes out the same if Jesus is not the foundation. We only have one source of home or fulfillment. We were not made to be under someone but alongside in love, united through Christ. God wants you eye to eye, not as a beggar.

Use Your Authority

Knowing our true identity reveals the authority we have in Christ. There is peace to all those on whom His favor rests (Luke 2:14). This simply means for all the saved and redeemed, there is peace from God through Christ's finished work. Jesus said to believe and make disciples by sharing Him. Never did He say to go and convert. There is no fruit on this earth for one who is saved but does not know what they have in Christ. Not knowing what we have is just like not having it at all. The devil uses what we do not know to fool and trick us. Whoever believes in Jesus will do the works He did and greater things than those (John 14:12). Speak to the mountain (the problem) and believe that what you say will happen, it will be done (Mark 11:23). Just believe when you speak it, see it in your heart, and look at it as finished afterward. See it in your heart (you're perfect, just like Jesus's born-again spirit). When we live by grace, we do better than we could ever even plan to do on our own. The beauty is sometimes we blink our eyes and realize from the rest, "Wow, this is better," or "I do not think about this anymore. It is just awesome, and I do not know how, but then I realize that is Jesus!" He died before we were born and sinned. That is love. The work on the cross has taken care of everything. You know there is no such thing as good luck. There is only blessing, and that has one source. The cross provided all of that. We even hear people saying "knock on wood" as a protection or good luck. This is empty and really silly when you think about it. I used to go along with that just because I heard it so much. I can choose faith in Christ or a piece of wood. However, look at this, truth is always revealed. Truth will absolutely always be revealed. This is because God is truth, and we always feel a drawing near to God. Even if people do not choose to walk in belief or start some untrue things like "knock on wood," God will always bring truth. The cross was wood. Catch that!

Remember, we are to live inside our spirit, soul, then body. Many of us do not even know we have a spirit. We are taught spirit and soul are interchangeable. This is how miracles and freedom from sin are missed. How can anything happen that God already provided if we do not even know we have the vessel to receive or if we are living from the wrong space? God is a spirit and must be worshiped and communed with from our spirit. The source of all good things in us is our perfect spirit that Jesus provided to us. We want that to pour out into our souls and bodies. Our body was made to serve us. That is not something we hear at all. Instead, we live mostly in fear of our bodies, letting them control us and even going to look for problems with them. When we do that, we are distracted from our relationship with God and, therefore, miss the most important part and the fruit of that. God provided authority over everything that sin brought through Jesus. Sin brought death, sickness, heartache, etc. Jesus brought all the good back, redemption, and more. Our body is to serve us, not we serve it. Money is also to serve us for the kingdom of God to be known to all, not for us to serve money. We are to serve the Lord only. Our purpose is to be God's, not the flesh. Churches will only be effective and the blessing they were made to be if we rely solely on the Lord for all things. People have stopped going to church because it is not the church Christ provided. They mistakenly think church is a building. It is God's people coming together anywhere. It must be all about Jesus. We have to individually receive all that Jesus did for us, share it, and live as the body of Christ. God being taken out of things or separated will lead to problems and defeat because He is the source of all good.

When it comes to healing, we have to realize that when we are saved, we already have it. Jesus took all of our sin on the cross. Sin brought death, disease, sickness, and sadness. He took all of that on his body for the past, present, and future as a one-time perfect sacrifice and atonement for our sin, not His. He took on the bad and released the good to us, which is forgiveness, healing of self, healing of others, divine health, and joy. We are to speak His finished work over ourselves and others. Jesus is the source of power. He died, and all sin and what sin brought was defeated and perished. He rose again on the third day, and all the redemption rose with Him. We are not to accept defeat, such as sickness. We are not to label ourselves with sickness and diagnoses of many kinds. The only label we are to have is saved of Jesus, the righteous ground where nothing bad can take residence. There can only be a good harvest on righteous ground. Jesus is all and enough. Do not believe the lie that we are still defeated.

There was a time in my life when I welcomed sickness. I was taught people just get sick and to expect that especially as we grow. Then I started noticing that was even a lie because I was seeing children and young adults sick and even dying. We are to grow stronger, not weaker. In the Old Testament, Caleb is mentioned as someone who gave his whole heart to God. He was in the same strength at eighty-five as he had been at forty years of age (Joshua 14:11). Moses climbed the mountain where he would die in full strength at one hundred and twenty years of age (Deuteronomy 34:7). He lived the number of his days because of the grace of God. He is so merciful that He made sure Moses saw the Promised Land even from afar despite the mistakes he had made. God loves us and does not place value on us or strength in us based on the number of years we have lived. Everything God sees is through Jesus, and we get to enjoy this beautiful and free gift of love that He provided to us all if we so choose to receive it and walk in it. This is sad, but in my own power, it felt safer to just accept defeat and sickness than to respond with the truth of God's Word and the finished work of Jesus. The thing to know and walk in is that we do not need to fight anything. We are not only already victorious in Jesus, but the fight for anything is over when we accept Jesus as our Savior.

Remember, we do not need to help God out. He already took care of everything. We should never take things into our own hands. There is an example in the Old Testament of someone trying to help God out as the ark of God was being brought back to Jerusalem. "When they came to the threshing floor of Nakon, Uzzah reached out and took hold of the ark of God, because the oxen stumbled" (2 Samuel 6:6). This man died because he was sinful trying to help God, who is perfect, and sin had its effect. God is to lead, and we follow, or it does not work. Just as now in the new covenant there are even many who are saved but live in defeat, have no effect, no fruit because we are not living as disciples who follow the Teacher. Instead, there are many who are converted and saved by Jesus, and that is it. Being saved is amazing but not all of God's plan.

We have authority and boldness. We need not pray as they did in the Old Testament. We do not beg and plead. We are to speak with authority to the problem, the authority we have in Christ. Prayer is thanking God for what He has already done and praising Him for who He is and what we now have as He intended all along. The beauty of God is He knows what you need before you do. He knows your heart and your thoughts. We do not need a speech for prayer. Personally, I cannot even tell a person I am praying for them anymore. It feels like an empty cliché. I tell them, "I speak over you." I have received some looks because many do not know the authority Jesus freely gave us all who believe in His finished work. There is no such thing as certain people are prayer warriors. Every believer has power because we receive that in Christ. It does not take a big group of people in order for God to do something. Yes, it is great, but not the only way. Jesus spoke clearly on how to use the authority that He provided and did not say it was first or only by the number of people praying. Prayer is thanking Him for what He has already done and appreciating that. It is not a speech or a time to beg and plead. Doing our part and living by faith in what He has provided is speaking over anything and speaking to the problem directly about your God and how Jesus already conquered it and provided the solution. We are not to sit there calling prayer, begging, or complaining about things God already knows about. He has already provided the solution to any problem we will ever face. We can also rest in the fact that God already knows the things you face. You do not have to waste energy sharing and complaining. That is one true connection like no other. It is faith in the Savior that brings forth what is already there. It is not the number of people or the amount of faith. It is simply believing we receive it before our physical eyes see it. If you need healing, you have it. Speak it, see it in your heart, and do things a healed person would do. One simple example of walking this out is if you are speaking for the healing of a knee, speak to the knee with the authority to work. Tell it God made it to work properly and Jesus already provided your healing. Take literal physical steps as one would with a proper working knee, believing it is finished. We cannot go by what we feel; we have to go by what we know. This comes from our born-again spirit. We are to speak to the problem "the mountain" about our God. Jesus does not have a bad knee. As He is, so are we in this world right now. Yes, facts can be proven. However, facts change all of the time. When a person is, in fact, sick, they refer to themselves as sick. When that same person is well, they refer to themselves as healthy. Even facts change all of the time. God and His Word never change or fail, not even once.

Our words are powerful. Our authority from Jesus comes by using our words. Let us speak life, not death. We must know what we are saying and not just follow others. The only one to be followed is Jesus. He already changed the world. Some just have not chosen to open the door to it. That is our part as believers to share that the door is there. Our tongue is a powerful tool in Christ to be used for Him. God is so good; if we are scared, it is not from Him. He gives us the solution to that, too. Just believe, do it afraid because He will not fail us, and He promises the fear will leave as it is already defeated. He gives us the gift to praise and worship Him through singing. If you are ever in a scary situation or just feeling fearful, know it is not God and sing!

About two years ago, I started experiencing feelings of fear of heights and driving. I had never been afraid of either one ever before. At one point in my life, I would have even loved to be a racecar driver as I have always liked racing and sports cars. One dream I have had is even driving the pace car for a race. Anyway, the fear started happening more and more. This is because I was not using my authority in Christ. I was just settling for it and getting through it, just getting by with it. Then, one day, I was at home and just saw so clearly that it was not from God. He revealed this to me and that the evil one will even disguise his lies as protection from God. I had even entertained the thought that I was scared because God was protecting me from something so I would not be somewhere I should not be. He will not scare us to help us. He lets us know which way we should go but does not scare us, so we do not. We have free will; He will not manipulate us. He is the truth. I decided to walk in this revelation that the evil one was just trying to get me to stop using the authority that I now knew I had in Jesus. I said no. We have to remember to tell Satan to get behind us. The evil one has no power; he is a defeated foe forever.

We cannot let him lie to us that he can affect anyone without their permission. The evil one wants us to be in a stagnant state, scared, and not be mobile in any way. I drive and drive up high bridges. God turns everything around for good. I only grew closer to Him from that as He whispered to me to look at the road with my eyes one piece at a time. I did and then literally felt a gentle hand behind my back guiding me with the most gentle touch. We are like the wheels; He is the motor. We will always be moving in a good and upward direction in peace.

Churches should not be appealing to others but being the love of Christ. If Jesus Himself did not walk this earth appealing but instead revealing, we should be following in this finished work. Hold to Jesus, not works. I speak that churches (the body of Christ) start trusting God again for provision and purpose. I even came across a church that had a gathering that involved beer and discussion of God. I had to look at it three times to believe that they were advertising beer and saying they were not "judgy" to get people to come. Stand in the faith and the foundation of Christ. I say this in love; they just did not realize what they were doing. I believe they had good intentions, just wrong information. Church is not supposed to be an advertisement but a blessing. We are supposed to welcome people to grace and let God's Word do what only His Word can do. Jesus already took care of everything. Alcohol impacts many families, so the topic of beer as part of this was unsettling. If we are embarrassed or scared to share Christ, just think, *I can only do this with the Holy Spirit*. Surely, we want Jesus to represent us to God. He is not embarrassed or scared. He conquered, so we should walk in that victory. There is nothing for us to conquer, just to share. We have authority in Christ that was freely given.

As I mentioned before, it was on our family's heart to find a church that preached the Bible, the fullness of Christ. We did not find it then. What we found was the leaders of the church we attended wanted the children to go to a children's program. Maybe that works for some, but it was not what we had in our hearts. My children did go once and wanted to be in church with us as they said they just danced to music. Children need to hear the Word. God's Word is for all. A child that is raised up in the Word will not flee from it. We are not supposed to just provide entertainment to children. They need His Word, too. It is okay if they act as if they do not want to hear it or do not understand. Seeds are being sown. It will always produce an abundant harvest. We need to stop thinking we need to entertain. We need to simply maintain our faith and let His Word do what only His Word can and will do every time. Remember, it is not about our works and that also means a child's attitude or behavior towards hearing the Word. It is important for families to hear His Word together as a church and at home. We need to remember church is not a building. It is God's people coming together. Even when it is a topic that may be uncomfortable, the fact is we should want our kids to hear it from a godly source, not the world. The truth is they will hear it somewhere. We live in this technology-filled world where things that children used to never see are right there on a screen, even popping up on children's shows or games. Children do not get to be children today with technology and phones in their hands and the devil a click away. Deuteronomy 11:1–7 talks about the fact that we need to share with our children and from generation to generation so His Word does not fade in their hearts. His Word never changes, but the receiver in people can be turned off or turned down. The children of each generation afterward did not see the good God had done.

We must keep passing it down and let it show from our hearts. "Teach a child the way he should go, and he will not turn from it" (Proverbs 22:6). We have the current state of the world because God is not shared, and He is even being taken out of things little by little. We have to hold to Him and His Word. He will always be your supply (Deuteronomy 11:22–25). Remember, the church is actually the believer coming together with other believers; the building is secondary. A church is the body of Christ and can gather outside and still be a church.

Speaking in tongues is not evil. I once thought it was because that is what I was taught. It even seemed scary because I had no understanding of it. What we do know can bless us. What we do not know can hurt us. We miss great blessings if we do not know the truth. Speaking in tongues is godly, and the Bible says so and describes the deep benefits of receiving the full gift of Christ. This gift comes from the baptism of the Holy Spirit, and it strengthens us. The second step after receiving Jesus is the baptism of the Holy Spirit. It is not with water. Jesus cleansed us. It is by invitation welcoming the Holy Spirit in your life to teach you and guide you until you close your eyes and are with the Lord or Jesus comes back first. God's Word gives instructions on speaking in tongues that remind us that it strengthens us as individuals. We are not all to speak in tongues all at once in a church gathering. If someone comes who is not saved yet, it is no good to them. They may even leave and think believers are out of their minds and still be lost. Speaking in tongues among others is to be done by no more than two or three, and one must be there to interpret so others can understand (1 Corinthians 14:27).

Remember, God's wrath against sin, not you, was settled with Jesus. He is most holy and perfect and could not be around anything evil, which is sin, and sin brings death. God is love and life. He is the author of honesty, too, and gave us free will. We must choose redemption through Jesus, not ourselves. People cause wars, and so does the enemy, just as sin brings death, separation, and sickness. Those who are not saved still have a corrupted spirit, and every piece of them is drawn to sin. They need love, grace, and mercy, just like we all do. Share it.

The enemy wants sin and destruction. We need our eyes opened to see who is truly behind this today: the devil. Weather is even called an act of God. Would God send His only Son to die for us and then send a storm to take a life? No, absolutely not. There is no more of God's wrath. Sin was atoned by Jesus. God never wanted anyone to suffer. His wrath was truth because He is life and perfect, and sin is death. God does not lie so He cannot be part of sin or around it. The body of Christ needs to be the body of Christ teaching and reaching with all our hearts.

We need to share that all who are saved have Christ-given authority and healing and that Jesus provided divine health and peace. We, as believers, are in the world, not of it. We are not to go by what is going on in this fallen world. We are to be the light so others can live the same life as a victor, not a victim. The enemy is a defeated foe who just lies and pretends he is not defeated. The truth is also he never had any power. People just submit to the enemy, believing lies because in the flesh, that seems easier because the flesh is sinful and likes sinful things. Think about the things we are willing to believe in the flesh or the things we will try because someone said it is a good idea. Yet, we do not trust God and His Word, which is always true and does not change. In this world, what was good yesterday can be called bad today. Trust God. There is no room for fear or fear of offense because the things of the world will pass away. God is always there forever.

Up until about one year ago, I did not know what a true blessing Communion is supposed to be. We are not supposed to practice a religious ceremony but come boldly and take Communion even in our homes to benefit us. This is for us to remember and keep walking in the fullness of Christ without distraction. This is not for God. It is for us. Jesus wants us to do this to remember what He did for us so that we continue walking in victory now and not just later. The works are provided through Jesus—the one true way. The gifts (blessings) are ours. The only thing we are to do is believe so we can rest and be blessed. Just receive. Let us stop trying to do more. Jesus labored so we can rest. It is what He did, not you. This is why we do not see miracles and people or creation walking in divine health. Yes, I said creation is not just people. Jesus said to go and share the good news with all creation. In different translations, it says creation, creature, and everyone, not just people.

Animals and nature yearn for the renewal of everything, too. The world is beautiful, but we do not see it in its perfection because of sin in this world. Sin affects everything. All of creation yearns for Jesus to return and make all things perfect again. Speak over everything with this knowledge. We must live knowing what we already have, not what we need to try and get. I repeat, it is not what you have to do because that is a major struggle for all of us. We live in a sinful world, and sin brings death and punishment. So even though when we believe in Jesus, we are set free and blessed with all blessings, we must renew our minds. We have to be in God's Word to learn to live from the spirit and change how we think so we do not even accidentally punish ourselves. God is a spirit, so this is a spiritual walk. If we try to do this from the flesh we think we have to earn our forgiveness or pay back a debt for it or that we can lose it when we make a mistake. Just receiving the one free gift is the thing to do and part of the journey of renewing our minds. Right now, while writing this book, I am still dying to myself. It is a walk. The world keeps being in our faces, saying, "Be all about yourself." There are many factors that come our way every day, trying to give self-life again. It does not matter if we stumble with this; dust it off and move on. That is the key. I am writing to remind myself who I am in Christ and why I am even doing this. It is okay; just be loved. That is the only thing we need to do. We cannot lose our authority in Jesus's name.

Communion is the bread that represents Jesus's broken body so we can be healed completely and live in a heart of love and divine health now and forever. The wine represents His blood shed for all of our sins so we are freed from the effects of sin forevermore. Sin was dealt with completely. He covered the sins of every single person. Forgiveness and redemption from sin were provided through Jesus. God is a spirit; we must worship in spirit. Communing with Him is not works by physical hands and ceremonial rituals. It is just being loved. This is how you commune and pray without ceasing. If you receive the baptism of the Holy Spirit, you can live in the fullness of Jesus's finished work. Otherwise, you will be saved only, which is wonderful, but not live the fullness of what He provided or the fullness of your days God intended. Yes, there are many who do not live the fullness of their days. The devil does not always have to work hard in this fallen world. It is by working on what we do not know we have as believers or preying on an unbeliever's loneliness and emptiness. This is oftentimes done through all the fear that is enforced by many commercials or advertisements on billboards. These methods of communication focus on some kind of problem or illness that is displayed to say you have to do something yourself. One of the evil one's main tactics is distraction, which is very easy in a technology-filled world where phones never stop beeping or ringing, even in a church service.

We only have our time on earth now to make the choice and choose redemption through what Jesus did, not what we do. He is the lampstand that brings light to us. Just a side note—in the Old Testament, a burnt offering represents sin forgiveness. A grain offering represents Jesus's broken body for our healing, and a fellowship offering represents our "old self" being crucified with Christ. All of this was pointing to Jesus before He came and saved us. We are not to make an image in the form of anything in heaven above or on the earth as far as the waters below (Deuteronomy 5:8). We were meant to live with Jesus in our hearts, which brings the choice of inviting the Holy Spirit to guide us and teach us the way. We are not to make statues of Jesus on the cross and bow down before them. God is a spirit and is as close as close can be within us in our hearts. We are to come boldly and not be afraid to walk up to the altar as if Jesus did not finish everything for us. I have been in churches where it was forbidden to come close to the altar unless you were certain people. Some of the churches also had statues of Jesus, Mary, and Joseph that we are not supposed to create and bow down to. Remember, Jesus did it all, not me, not you, or a priest. We receive grace, a free gift that has nothing to do with our works. Come boldly and receive the fullness of Christ. It is not what God wanted that many believers have left us and got to heaven and then found out how wonderful God is. He does not want us to find out in heaven that we had authority that He gave us through Jesus the whole time and never used it. What matters is they were saved and made it there. However, He wants us to know Him now. We are not to limit God like that.

We need to pass the memo of how great He really is and that He is for all and waiting for all to accept Jesus and come back to Him. We are to use our Christ-given authority to speak healing over others. Jesus said to share that the kingdom of heaven has come near. He tells us to go and heal the sick, raise the dead, cleanse those that have leprosy, and drive out demons. He freely gave so we could freely receive (Matthew 10:7–8). We are to freely share with all what we have, and it is for all to receive, too. Leprosy represented punishment and the curse sin brought. Jesus frees us from the punishment, curse, separation, and loneliness of sin.

We are also not to keep grieving for the saved that have passed; they are in perfection. Yes, we miss them, but they are with God. We need to focus on passing on His truth so others can have Him now and forever. The focus is on others receiving this free gift. If we focus on sharing Christ with others so they do not perish, we will not be afraid to do so if we think what will happen if we do not. "For my yoke is easy and my burden is light" (Matthew 11:30). There is no one who goes to heaven without accepting Jesus.

Think about that. Just share, we have the most important job because we do not want anyone to suffer for eternity. We want others to have a life now and forever. I am writing this book to you that all started when my husband purchased a Bible and had my name engraved on the cover. He did not even read the Bible at the time. God used him. He had no idea what he did for me. The Bible that I could not touch as a child was given to me in a smaller version, pink, and had my name engraved on it. Remember, I had been taught that the Bible was big and not to be touched. Now, I had one just for me. What he gave me, he had no clue. The fact that it was pink with even my name put on it was God speaking to me to come near. He was telling me I am His child and that He does not use big, scary things. He uses the things the world would not. He uses things that will glorify Him, reach others, and lift them up.

The world teaches us to be self-sufficient. Even people who appear so powerful are not. The only power comes from God. We only have power through Jesus. God made us to live life with Him not without Him. Because we are born into sin, we live life backward from what He intended. We live from the outside first, our flesh. Sin flips everything backward. We were created to live by our spirit. However, when sin entered the world, our spirit was not full of life anymore because it became corrupted by sin. Our nature became sinful and not right with God. So, we are all first dominated by our physical bodies and feelings, which is the opposite of how God made us to live.

The good news is He is truth. He does not lie. He gave us all free will. One sin was committed that brought the fall and corrupted us all. However, He found a way when there seemed to be no way for Him to have His people back. This is through Jesus. When we are born again, there is no guilt, just peace. Guilt and fear are never from God. God does not condemn. He convicts. All this means is that He lets us know when we need to turn away from something because it is sin. Just turn back and keep walking in the forgiveness provided to you. Remember, Jesus died once and only once for all of our sin, past, present, and future.

See It

When Adam and Eve started existing in sin, their spiritual eyes were closed, and they were bound only by what they could see with their physical eyes. God is merciful; we have an imagination to see things in our hearts before we see them in the physical. We must picture things first on the inside of us before they can be in the natural. If we do not believe to the point of seeing it in our imagination, how can it come to be? See yourself well, talk about being well, and do things that a well-doing person would do. Andrew Wommack taught me about imagination. God gave us an imagination to see things from our spirit and to move about in this world, like remembering how to get home or drive to a store. We have the imagination to see first inside of us what God has provided so then we can see it on the outside in the physical. This is how we cross the barrier that sin brought.

Jesus is the door to make this possible. We have to see it inside of us first. From our spirit, we can see what God sees. We need to see in our hearts Jesus taking in all the darkness on the cross and then releasing His light to all people. When He said, "It is finished," picture seeing all of His light being released to you. Sin, death, and sickness were dealt with forever—just receive. It is all in what we believe. This world is still fallen and full of sin and lies. The saved are no longer fallen but redeemed from the curse that sin brought. May the God of hope fill you with all joy and peace as you trust in Him so that you may overflow with hope by the power of the Holy Spirit (Romans 15:13). It matters what we focus on. What we are focused on is where we will be, we must see and focus on His goodness always.

Signs are everywhere about being sick, checking for sickness, and being aware of sickness. Insurance companies are now advertising everywhere. I have even heard of there now being four forms of a disease that became a diagnosis not so long ago. Awareness has become a word used so much and people come together based on that word. The only awareness that is going to save you or solve a problem is knowing we need Jesus and receiving His goodness. Otherwise, we are going in circles, getting worse if anything, and just coming together to make the circle bigger instead of living a fruitful and victorious life. The flesh loves the word awareness and rare like a rare disease. The devil is having a party because people are coming together for anything but God instead of the body of Christ having its full effect. Be careful for nothing. This means being anxious for nothing and just trusting to rest. It is already done. Choose to walk in it.

Let us start having conversations about life, not death, what is right, not wrong in our lives. Let's do nice things for one another again, give a compliment to someone. Receive the gift of love and a warm heart—true kindness, not a cold heart. God does not give us troubles. I have heard more than once that God gives big things and big problems to those He trusts most. That is all about self. God loves us so much to know that He cannot trust us. He trusts Jesus. He who's finished work has made us new in Him. We have more available to us when we receive the Holy Spirit, His Spirit, to teach and guide us. God shows no favoritism (Romans 2:11). He trusts in the finished work of Christ, who wiped all sin away. If we receive Jesus, we have all of His benefits and blessings given to us. It is not at all about us and our works. God just loves us and made the one way back to Him—

Jesus. Believe and receive. You will be blessed with no doubt. We are growing all the time. The growth will not stop until Jesus comes back and we receive our glorified bodies as God first intended for us. If we do not teach this and do not tell this truth, we get many people not receiving what God had for them. We think way too small anyway. Our greatest dreams are God's starting point. God is wonderfully big and full of love. As Jesus is, so are we in this world (1 John 4:17). We now have a boldness because of Jesus. We are not to beg God and talk to Him as if He is far away. The Holy Spirit is His Spirit within us, teaching, guiding, protecting, and loving us every step of the way if we choose to give Him permission. As Jesus is, He is whole, strong, healthy, powerful, has all authority, and wants us to use this that He gave us. We have it now in this world, not later in heaven.

    I also cannot say with good thought to tell someone to be careful. In this world, we use clichés or say things we do not really think about what they mean just because we heard it before over and over from whoever. The Bible says to be careful for nothing. When we say be careful, we are saying be anxious. Yes, by worldly standards, it is kind and caring. The Lord has us. We need not worry about anything, and we need to be aware it is not us that saves us or keeps us safe. It is the Lord and His finished work. This thinking requires saying no to pride. This world does not teach this. In the world, everything is said to be about self, which is death, not life. There are many people who lived eighty years, never truly living, and had the mindset they were just dying slowly year by year. That is not God. When you have Jesus, death is behind you. Live inside out, and there is life in the spirit that is perfect just like Jesus.

    Speaking in tongues is also such a strengthening to us that God loves us because our spirit is praying while we rest in faith. Faith is all God ever asked for because faith is our love back to God. The only wrong way to pray is to beg and ask God to move when it is we who need to move by faith. The power of God comes through Jesus; He is

God's, and we are His. We are reunited through the love of the Father for His Son and the love of His Son for His people. Our authority is through the door, Jesus, so we may not boast. God gets the glory because He is the source. We are to be a usable vessel. We will always be blessed by that. To give God the glory is to be blessed forever. Boasting is empty and leads to destruction every time. Certain things are absolute. If it is not God, an absolute every time is failure, and destruction will happen if He is not the foundation. Miracles seemed to not happen for some people or seem to not happen as they once did because people quit believing and speaking as Jesus said to do. It became about us instead of Him. We cannot do anything, and miracles cannot happen without the source that is Jesus.

I hear and read God moves by faith. However, God is not still moving; He is resting and waiting. He created everything we would ever need in six days and rested the seventh. He put the seed for all things in the earth to be fruitful and multiply during creation. He made the way for Jesus. On the cross, before Jesus gave up His spirit, Jesus said, "It is finished" (John 19:30). Catch this. Instead of us trying to get God to move, it is truly by faith that we receive what He has already provided. Faith opens the door. Jesus provided all redemption, and He also rest. It is all already there; we just have to choose to take and receive it. Please see the difference. We can only have if we know the grace He provided to us before we were even born.

Time is for us when things do not happen right away. God is so merciful; He will not rush things that are meant as a blessing. He is not bound by time. However, He knows in this sinful world that we are bound by it. This is why no one knows the hour Jesus will come back. God wants everyone to have a chance and a choice to choose Him. He gave us free will to choose to receive. We do this by faith, knowing it is already there and seeing it in our hearts first. This is how He made things work, so even though we have free will, His protection is still available. He wants us to be ready so the blessing is received and does not become a curse to us instead. The hardest thing to do is to submit to God and rest which is living in faith. This is the only way and the only thing we must do as believers. We struggle so much because of the flesh that is so active in this world. We want achievement and self-recognition in the flesh. It is right there, and we can feel the flesh first. Achievements on our own will never last. We cannot go by what we feel; we have to go by what we know.

Remember that the flesh in this world is corrupted and drawn to sin. We must renew our minds to live inside out in this current world. We have to see things from the inside out, not from the outside in. This means living by our spirit by faith, not our flesh. We do not have a first and only direct connection to the spirit. We can only access it through faith, knowing it is there. Believers already have the victory. We cannot live by circumstances because we still have our flesh that is competing for our attention. It is truly so easy if we just believe, rest, and stop making it about ourselves. The flesh is not the way we are to live in this world; it is by faith that we know our spirit is there and live by it first. Our first and only connection will not be our spirit until we receive our glorified bodies. For now, we live this way by faith because we are made righteous through Christ. However, the world has not been freed from sin yet. There is still a barrier between flesh and spirit because of this. Through Jesus, the barrier between God and us is gone, and we now only have a barrier from our spirit to our flesh. However, now that we have authority we can choose to let our spirit flow to our soul and then our body and have the benefits of the spirit to all parts of us. The barrier that was between us and God has been made to be truth and protection for our spirit forever. Righteousness cannot be where sin is because God, who is righteousness, cannot be where sin exists. Through Jesus, we now have righteousness in our spirit that reunites us with God and completely redeems us in spirit, soul, and body. Jesus turns the barrier sin brought to our spirit around for good and uses that barrier to protect our perfect spirit forever. Our perfect spirit that is full of life-giving water now flows and becomes one way—outward. It can only pour out into our souls and bodies and then to others. Nothing bad, no sin can touch our spirit ever again. The barrier will no longer be there when we receive our glorified bodies because there will be no sin around us, no protection needed, and no separation of any kind. We will be fully aware of our spirit first and only. We will not feel any pain or anything that is not good. For now, this is why we speak to the problem in the authority of Jesus about our God and who He is. Our flesh still currently exists around sin, which brings negative surroundings and negative effects. Jesus freed believers from this now and forever. It is just accessed by faith right now. That is all. Just know that a believer's perfect born-again spirit is there, and be blessed.

See it in the spirit. Again, God created everything and provided everything we would ever need in six days and rested in perfection on the seventh day. Jesus came into this world years later and finished everything that sin brought after the fall. God is excited and waiting, and Jesus is seated at His right hand. Remember, He is seated—resting and waiting. Should we not rest? Living by the spirit and letting the living water flow to our souls and bodies and then out to others is all we need to do and how we rest. It is not being still physically and not moving. It is being at peace in our hearts that everything is done and sharing that with others. Faith is a movement in our spirit. However, it is more restful than just sitting there doing nothing physically with our bodies. If you notice, we are always set to be moving and rising upward from our spirit.

It is not what goes in; it is all about what comes out that affects our lives. We have the freedom to choose. Everything was and will always be meant to flow from our spirits. Our hearts can only be good and good forever with Jesus. He is the author of redemption and new birth. Being born again and then welcoming and receiving the baptism of the Holy Spirit is what gives us the fullness of Christ. Water baptism is a public display. It does not do anything for God. It is letting others know who your life belongs to. If not careful, this starts a works mentality.

Jesus said to go and baptize them in the name of the Father, the Son, and the Holy Spirit because we need all three. This is God our Creator and Father, Jesus our Savior and Friend, and the Holy Spirit our Teacher and Comforter—our guidance. Jesus was baptized in water to represent our sins being washed away by Him and being made new, which could only be by what He did, not what you do, including getting water baptized. If you do and feel a pull to get baptized in water also—great! Trust and follow Him only. I had a completely different experience of trying to, and it never worked because my heart was wrong, and I thought I had to do this—me! God revealed to me that it is about what Jesus did, not some ceremonial thing I do. Everyone's journey is not the same. What is the same is His Word. God's Word has to be it and enough. If His Word says it, that is what I am standing on and nothing else.

When you submit your life to Christ, sometimes people turn away. It is a blessing, not a curse. People in darkness turn away from light because it is too bright. It is just like going out in the sun without sunglasses. We will turn away and look down. The people who turn away could be immediate family; it has happened in my life. However, God's Word is true and will never return void. His Word comes to pass if we just believe. We will absolutely never regret it. Jesus said no one who puts a hand to the plow and looks back is fit for service in the kingdom of God (Luke 9:62). Only when we follow Him and do not look back at the past, who or what we think we lost, is when we find the true life God had planned for us from the beginning. If we are still looking back, we have not submitted our life to Him. Do not look back; He has you covered in all directions. Submit to God, and the wrong doors will close, and the right doors will open. He is a giver, not a taker. In the Old Testament, He was always giving knowing the people would fail. We no longer have failure because of Jesus. Every door that closes, God promises another will be opened and another and another to where there are more open doors than one could have ever imagined. It is a snare of the devil to live by circumstances. A believer resides in the finished work of Christ; speak to the problem about your God. Speak to the mountain, "the problem," by faith, as Mark 11:23 says, and it will fall every time. See it in your heart that the victory is yours.

We have an innate longing that no one can deny in truth that we long for God and know we need Jesus's redemptive work, not our own. We desire acceptance. The problem is the world twists that to acceptance coming from people. Acceptance can only come from God and through Jesus. We all long to be loved, to love others, and to get along with others. There is only one source of that—Jesus. We hear over and over that someone is searching for who they are or to find themselves, even sometimes taking trips and alone. This should be a red flag because getting us alone is a sneaky tactic of the devil. He wants to get a lonely person alone and away from any support to destroy them. We were not made to be alone. A born-again believer is never alone ever again! Christ is our one true identity, our home, and our peace. Always go where there is peace, whether it is literally a place or a decision. Peace is only found in Christ. He is the only true source.

Anything that is not through Jesus is a lie and will fail every time. Jesus defeated the enemy. He has given us everything to not be powerless to the devil or be harmed by the enemy. He makes it clear that we are to rejoice that we are part of His kingdom, not just focus on the power we have to do the things He did (Luke 10:18–19). The power through Him is a beautiful extra but not the foundation. It is the eternal kingdom. The true gift is not power but the gift of eternal life. The power is just part of the way because He loves us and wants us to share and reach others. Our victory is in Christ. This world yearns for power that is always absolutely lost every time. Power is empty without the source of love and purpose. God is the only true source. We all need Him. We all fail to meet the needs of others. God does not. Let Him be your source so you are full and can fill others. That is what the kingdom of God is all about—love. The body of Christ is to spread that love. God will never fail you even once. He is always there. The Israelites were always looking for a king. There is no king except Jesus. You do not have to wait for this. He is there already. Receive. The name of Jesus is repeated because His name is everything. He is the only answer to all things and the only source of power and authority. It is really this simple.

To live the fullness of our days is only found in submission to God and resting in Christ, as God is the one who wrote the number of our days before we were born. The sad part is many are not living that number because they are listening to other things and trying to do what has already been done and could only be successfully done through Christ. There are more signs than ever about problems, mainly health problems. Look at what is on the internet or social media. It could be used for good, but unfortunately, that is not common. We are what we hang around, including the internet and advertisements we allow around us. The world teaches us that forty years of age is old. There is no old in the kingdom of God. There is just forever. Forty has been a symbolic and repeated number that has brought strength, change, and new growth closer to God. Some examples are the Israelites wandering in the wilderness for forty years by their own choice to be ready to possess the Promised Land. Noah was on the ark for forty days and forty nights, waiting for the flood to subside and to start again. Moses went up on Mount Sinai for forty days and forty nights to receive the Ten Commandments to point us to the truth that we need Jesus to save us from sin. Jesus was in the wilderness for forty days where He was tempted by the enemy. There were forty days between the crucifixion of Jesus and His ascension to heaven. This is when the Holy Spirit came. We need to see that God did not make anyone to grow old. Instead, He made us grow closer to Him and, therefore, get stronger.

Grades and college are not all there is to life. Grades started out with good intentions until we made them a god and set one main standard of learning for all. College was a good idea until we made that a god and spread the lie that this is how someone is somebody. We replaced Jesus with this, and many other things have been treated as gods. There is one true God. I am hearing more than ever that people change their careers completely or move somewhere else. This is not going to solve the problem. Jesus will. Also, if we are taught the truth that God's purpose for our lives is to first be loved then everything else will flourish from this one thing. Many of us would not still feel empty with even three college degrees. We would not be in the wrong places at the wrong time. As a result, God's purposes are not being fulfilled. What is happening is man is short-changed, and even completely wrong deeds are being carried out instead of God's plans. Our identity is not in the things we do or our careers. College is not an identity. It is a dot on a map for one who is called to truly be there. You know we do need craftsmen and other vocations as well.

We cannot or should not all be one thing. God loves us all equally. We all have an individual purpose to fulfill the kingdom. Honestly, all the prestige that is given to things that Jesus has already taken care of does not make much sense when you think about it. That is the devil; the name of the game is distraction and confusion. If you know the truth, you have a responsibility to share, as is why I am here doing something I really would not have chosen or thought would be in my path. We cannot all be the same part of the body of Christ. Then, the body will not work.

It is all about trust. Living for Christ is moving in peace even in the dark, knowing He is the light that will guide you always, even one little step at a time. Personally, I have experienced peace beyond understanding, and my life has not been predictable by any means since I submitted my life to Him. I have never been more fulfilled, loved, at peace, and excited about life and life eternal. We have a responsibility to share once we know, just like when the law was given, then sin was imputed to us. None of us follow all the Ten Commandments. Hello, it all points to Jesus, my dear friend. I say hello because that is what I said when I realized it. The truth is we cannot; only Jesus could do it. Now, believers have what we needed all along, so we must share the victory that is in give and receive.

Children are not held responsible for not being saved. However, the truth will set them free. God does not design and determine any child to die young. It is and always is the devil, and people unknowingly submit to this in the flesh. Any child who has died is with the Lord eternally. The truth is that God is good no matter what. Yes, there are many who have died before they were intended to. Remember this: they are in perfection. They could receive no more perfect gift. Premature death is not God's plan, but He will always turn anything around for good. In this life, we should not keep the fullness of Christ away from anyone and that includes a child. Raise them up so that they may bless the world with Christ.

God's Word will always provide what we need in absolutely any moment or situation. Psalm 91 came alive to me after my daughter fell off a horse. God brought me to this scripture after it happened. It was a beautiful day that day. My daughter, who was six years old at the time, was riding her favorite horse that she was so connected to. The horse spooked, and my daughter tried to stay on as the horse reared up a couple of times and then bolted. She fell off. However, it was so odd for me because I had this supernatural sense of peace before, during, and after it happened. It all seemed to happen in slow motion, and she did not slam on the ground. It is like she seemed to hover to the ground. My son, who was nine at the time, was quiet the whole time, which I did not notice until I thought back on it. My daughter's trainer ran to pick her up while the horse was on the other end of the outside arena. The horse was still galloping everywhere. Her trainer lifted her over the fence to me.

I felt such peace and hugged her tight. I just knew she was fine. Words cannot express the peace. I looked at her from head to toe anyway, as a mom would naturally do, just to take in her precious sight. I told her, "Well, you rode, fell off, ate dirt, and sat in the wildflowers all in one day." We had a big laugh, and her only concern was the horse. Her trainer got the horse, and my daughter walked her inside the barn, untacked her, and just kept patting her, asking her if she was okay. We left and stopped at a gas station because I just needed to sit for a minute, and she told me that she just cared if the horse was okay. My son then tells me, plain as day with eyes right on me in such peace, "Momma, there were two angels that held her." I cried and realized I already knew before I knew. Wow! Psalm 91:11–12 says that He will command His angels concerning you to guard you in all your ways; they will lift you up in their hands so that you will not strike your foot against a stone. You see, children seem to see these things more than adults because of their purity of heart, their innocence, and their lack of hardness in their hearts. We can all have a heart to see if we just choose freedom in faith.

The world twists what growing up actually is intended to be. It is not being self-sufficient; it is knowing who God is and knowing we need Him in all ways. Israel wanted another sinner to be over them as king. Then, there were times when they had no king to rule over them and did what they saw fit. Neither would work. We need the one true, sinless, perfect leader of love that is Jesus. In Judges, there is a mention of giving thanks to God and showing Him respect by making an image dedicated to Him. Then, the people would worship that. God clearly said not to do this. They were living in the flesh and wanted to see something with their physical eyes to the point that they would worship something that they had to make and did not move or do anything for them. They thought it was by their works as well. They went against what God clearly said. God is a spirit and is to be worshiped in spirit.

The Israelites spent forty years in the desert and countless other years of problems and loss because they would not listen and wait by faith. The wait was for them to be ready. God had already provided what they needed. We are to listen and wait by faith and come boldly expecting because what we need is already there. We have all we need already because of Jesus. He now rests at our Father's right hand because it is finished. He provided us with the chance for a brand-new perfect spirit if we accept Him in our hearts. God gave us His Spirit to guide us if we choose to invite Him to do so. We wait by faith now, even in the finished work of Christ, because God loves us so much. He wants us to be blessed, not cursed. In the Old Testament, God dwelled in the ark of the covenant, or the Israelites would go to a high place away to hear from God. Note the separation of God and man. It was a must because God cannot dwell amongst sin. Notice that the Israelites were always headed in an upward direction when they were seeking God. A blessing becomes a curse by our own choice when we are not ready. That is something that has only gotten worse today. People struggle to wait at a red light or in a drive-thru line. Waiting is a blessing. It builds us up every time, no matter the circumstance. Part of faith is waiting and believing without seeing. No one would or ever will benefit from never waiting. All that will happen is one will realize they did not even really want what they have or think there must be more than this. That is always the result because the thought that there must be more than this is our innate longing for Jesus, a redemption with God. This can only come by faith, waiting, and submitting our life to His beyond our understanding of His goodness. "For by one sacrifice, he has made perfect forever those who are being made holy" (Hebrews 10:14). This is the longing we search for: Jesus. He is the one perfect sacrifice. Where we have been forgiven by accepting Jesus as our Savior, any other sacrifice is no longer necessary (Hebrews 10:18). It is once and forever. There is no doing this more than once and rededicating our life to Christ. Once we are His, we are His forever. The reason we see pastors or other people talking about rededication is because they are not in His Word and in the guidance of the Holy Spirit. If we read the Bible, it is plainly said that we need to accept Jesus and welcome the Holy Spirit to teach and guide us. Then we have the guidance of Him leading us and not ourselves. We will see fruit this way and only this way. We must welcome the Holy Spirit to guide our lives.

Water baptism was done before Jesus died for us. John the Baptist baptized Jesus with water as a symbol of Him making us clean and washing away our sin (filth). Jesus did not have any sin to be cleansed from Himself. It is about what Jesus did and finished, not us adding or imitating what only He could do. Living as He does is about resting in Him, receiving what He could only provide, putting that to use, and then sharing this good news with others. We accept Jesus in our hearts to receive the gift of His perfect spirit making ours perfect. As He received the Holy Spirit before He began His ministry, we are given the Holy Spirit. The gift and the walk were not intended to be done without the Holy Spirit's guidance. God does not force so we need to then welcome the Holy Spirit to guide and teach us. After Jesus's death and resurrection, He received the ability to provide the Holy Spirit (God's Spirit with all believers). This is the part that is missing and why we do not see fruit like miracles as we should. It is there. We must know what we have already, open the gates, and turn our receiver on so it flows to our souls and bodies and out to others. This is what Jesus meant when He said to go and make disciples and baptize them in the name of the Father, Son, and Holy Spirit. We receive what Jesus completed and are not asked to do extra or take all the steps he took before He provided the gift. The gift is just that, a gift, a gift of grace and completely free of our doing. Just receive.

Jesus is the living bread that came down from heaven; manna was sent down from heaven before, and the people still died. He is the bread of life, when we receive, we live forever (John 6:47–51).

It is a blessing to see angels or other miraculous things with our physical eyes, but what is lasting is faith. That is knowing these things are real without seeing them in the physical and just knowing them in our hearts. The devil will even try to tell someone that something is not real, or people start focusing on seeing it again, and the devil is just distracting yet again. Let us stay focused and stay focused on faith in Jesus. Trying to see things in the physical world will not fulfill us like faith will in this fallen world. Yes, what I felt emotionally (soul) and physically (body) and what my son literally saw was amazing and a blessing. Both he and I have talked, expressing, yes, it is amazing, but we cannot just stay there because that is limiting God. He loves us, and His works are more amazing than we can comprehend. Let us appreciate and keep walking by faith because there is no limit to His goodness. As He is, so are we in this world (1 John 4:17). In all situations, we should not go by what we feel but by what we know. God's Word is true, and we need to know what His Word says so we can see it in our hearts first. All we have to do is stand on His Word. The Bible says that through Jesus I am saved and redeemed from all sin and what sin brought. That is what I am standing on, not what I see or what someone tells me.

Who we are is not the religion we classify as or those certain practices we follow. The only name that we are to hold on to is the name of Jesus. Our classification is a believer who is the saved of Jesus. We are not to be religious. We are to be believers in Jesus and only follow what He said for us to do. Then, we have found our one true identity for the first time. Religion is separation from God and people. Believers are blessed with everything that only Jesus could provide. We are blessed with the true victory now and forever. We are redeemed from everything sin brought. Religion and the certain practices that come with that separate us from what we have or keep us distracted from what we know. Religion does not build us up, works get involved, and we once again think we are low to God and lower than Jesus and have no authority that He freely shared with us. Jesus chose us. He calls us friends, no longer servants (John 15:15). Anyone who is not saved has not found their identity yet because it is received through Jesus only. For those who are saved, if religion is practiced and we do not just focus on Jesus, we are not walking in what He provided to us. Religious denominations bring us away from Jesus. "De" literally means to move away from. Different denominations came about because the truth of God's Word did not get passed along to others. Also, there have been those who were told and did not choose to believe in His Word and Jesus alone or agree with it, so then we now have different religious denominations. This is empty. God loves us and sees us through Jesus. We must receive Jesus to be saved and walk in His love. Then, the door is open to God, who is already there because Jesus died for us all. We just have to choose to open the door that is only found in Jesus. It is not supposed to be what the church has set up as their beliefs. The church is not supposed to choose the parts they want and do not want. The church is supposed to stand on what God's Word says and what His Word says we have because of Jesus. The one true church is the body of Christ. Everything stands on God's Word. If not, it will always fall. Please know the victory is already there. We do not have to be afraid because God would not ask us to do something that we cannot do. We do not have to be afraid to offend people, to speak in the authority we have in Jesus, or to speak on certain topics. The only thing we need to do is share Christ with our words and actions by sharing His love. Let the finished work of Jesus take care of problems and cover topics that people do not want to touch. Just share His love, not judgment. He did not judge us so that we would not be judged. Sin is sin, and righteousness is righteousness. Good cannot be good where bad exists. Every one of us needs Jesus to be saved. We are not better than anyone else. Jesus will always take care of everything with a promise. He has taken care of things that we cannot and should not. We must rely on Jesus, not ourselves. Our identity will never be found in the church building we go to. It is in Christ alone. Otherwise, someone will always be searching for who they are and never find it because God's Word does not lie or return void ever! His Word points to Jesus, not church buildings. I have been to churches that try to make people be who the church organization wants them to be, not just let Jesus's finished work have its full effect. We have to allow this to happen, then it always will. There are clicks and people looking down at others. Even one of the twelve disciples, John, told Jesus that they saw one driving out demons in Jesus's name, and they tried to stop him because he was not one of them. Jesus said not to stop him because whoever is not against you is for you (John 9:49–50). We need the church to be all about Jesus, trusting God will provide, and be a place for community and support. Instead, there is a holding tight of man's tradition and rules and people not knowing God's Word. So, the devil uses that. The true struggle is not between man but man's rules, traditions, and the enemy's tactics that bring pride. Remember, Jesus conquered it all. Tradition and rules of worship only distract us from God, make it about us and our works, and do not reach Him.

When we see creation, do you realize this is not even as beautiful as it really is? Sin in this world affects everything. We still live in a fallen world. It is those who accept Jesus who are saved, not the whole world made new just yet. It is an individual choice. Still, we say how beautiful things are. Although, let us remember to thank the Creator not worship those things. We are not to worship but appreciate the beauty in the sun, moon, stars, and events that take place as these things carry out their purpose and all of creation as a whole. We worship nothing else but the Lord.

I was taught not to share God with anyone and that we should not push Him on anyone. I was told that it is personal and not our business. Obviously, that was all the wrong information. At the time, I did not know except what I was told because I was not in God's Word. Later, I learned from my children about Jesus and that He is to be shared. When you have Him and not religion, you cannot help but share, even if just in your actions. He is so good that when you look to Him, you will truly be resting because you blink and realize *wow, I do not do this anymore. Wow, I do not watch or listen to that anymore.* My children are the ones who found Christian TV. We had canceled cable and then satellite because it was just too expensive. I look back on it now, and it was really because we were longing for better and not wanting to see what was on there. We now had eyes to see, and we had to turn from it. We put an antenna up on the house and had to reprogram the TV. My children had a receiving heart and found the channel SMILE, which is a Christian Television station for children. I would not have noticed. Then it went from there. That is all they wanted to watch.

Then we later came across worship music and started listening to that and that is what we listen to in different genres. That is where it is peaceful. At one point, we were trying to sell our house. My children asked me to keep SMILE on so it could bless whoever came into the house. I remember feeling uncomfortable as I was still growing and renewing my mind to the fact that we must share. I listened to their request even though I was so uncomfortable. I am thankful because I personally grew from that moment. People who would come to view the house mentioned the house being peaceful. God is God and never fails. When we renew our minds, a lot of change occurs in peace.

One will never want to go back. We cannot. Once the door to Jesus is opened, and we keep growing to know what he provided to us, the only way is up. We have eyes to see. He provides the living water that has a one-way flow forward. Things cannot help but get better. Even if circumstances are not good, we have peace because

He is above circumstances. A believer no longer lives according to the world. If we try, we will feel like we are in a land we do not know. We cannot help but change because Jesus brings the change. He brings us to God, away from the ways of the world. It is not work for us. To accept Christ is to humble ourselves, knowing we cannot save ourselves. We will do great things and not even be aware at first because we are resting in Jesus. "For all those who exalt themselves will be humbled, and those who humble themselves will be exalted" (Luke 14:11). If God gets the glory, then it is right.

Worshiping in spirit is living, knowing He is with you, carrying you along. There is truly no need to throw our hands up anymore unless you are not born again. Throwing our hands up is a physical sign of "I surrender; come to me." For the believer, He is there; let us act like it. We do not go searching for something that is already there or found. If we do not live like this that is why even believers feel like God is so far away. He is to be worshiped in spirit, your born-again spirit to His Spirit. He is right there, not in other things or that are far away in heaven. He loves you first; that is why He sent His only Son to die for you even before you were born. I have learned through the teaching of Joseph Prince that God blesses you even before you repent. He loves you first. Be forgiven. There is no painful toil when it is God and not our pride (Proverbs 10:22). The blessing comes before anything else. The first greatest blessing and the door is Jesus Christ and what He did for all of us. You know Andrew Wommack taught me through his teachings to look at the word pride. The letter "i" is right in the middle, and we all—every single one of us—have to surrender pride to live in Christ. We want to make everything about "I"—I have to do; I have to believe more. No, rest. Let us put Jesus in the center and rest. Friend, you will never control things and never have. To lose the lie that you do is to gain Christ.

When everything, and I mean everything in my life, made no sense, the truth came to light about everything in my life at the time. My life seemed to be destroyed. Everyone and everything I thought I knew outside of my husband and children was gone. The truth is I never had it. So many things had been based on lies that I believed. This is when I found Christ and found life for the first time. My prayer for you is that you find Him, too. I have had this beautiful pull, "a sweet spot," to share this because it is never too late. I firmly believe we will see an abundance of people begin their lives in these truths because the reality is God never plans for us to have it hard, fall, or have anything bad. It is because of not having the truth that we do because we choose to walk in lies even without knowing it. We can only go by what we know. If all we know is a lie, then that is what we are going to walk in. I was also told praying in tongues is evil when the Bible (if we actually read it) clearly states it is a gift from God that is the nearest and dearest and easiest way to communicate, commune, and have our perfect just like Jesus's spirit pray for us along with the Holy Spirit. This is strengthening for us and even rest while we talk to God. The devil wants everyone to be deceived. Praying in tongues is powerful, and the devil does not want us to know we have any power, much less use it.

Our relationship with God is first. It is the root. His Word is an incorruptible seed. Jesus is the living water that gives life to the seed, and knowing God loves us gives it roots to stand. A tree cannot stand without a root, just as nothing in the soil can grow and survive without strong roots. Andrew Wommack has said that if you have no root, the first problem you face, "your tree," will just fall over. This is why we need to renew our minds in the Word and put our relationship with God first. Reading the Word is for us, not God. He is not counting our works. See God's love and see Jesus when you read the Bible. Everything is accomplished and finished because of Christ. If we see this in our hearts and just receive it, then we will have some deep roots to bear fruit and share with others like our children. First, it is the renewing in us, sharing with our family, and then the world. You need good roots to stand. We cannot let the

Word fade in our hearts; that is why we need to read daily for our benefit. Otherwise, we will put people and their opinions over God. Our "field" will sprout weeds that way instead of fruit. Remember, God cares about your motivation, not the things you do. So even if your heart is to read the Bible every day and something comes up, and you cannot, just rest. Reading His Word is a blessing, not a chore or a checklist. Our hearts just need to be with His Word, not the world. We cannot live by the flesh and negative things in our ears constantly. We all have a choice. Jesus had to understand who He was and what He had before He died on the cross. This is the same for us learning who God is and who we truly are in Christ and that everything good only comes from Him. God is always there ahead, in the middle, and behind us covering us entirely in His amazing love. God is a spirit. Jesus is God's Spirit with a human body (fully God and fully man), and the Holy Spirit is God's Spirit available to be within us as our guidance. All we must do is put our faith in Jesus and welcome the Holy Spirit in our lives, who teaches and guides us in truth, not worldly lies. There is no recorded miracle done by Jesus until He received the baptism of the Holy Spirit. We have the same opportunity. Jesus said go and do as He did, and greater the works we will do (John 14:12). He said this because not only do we have His finished work—a perfect born-again spirit—we also have the choice to welcome the Holy Spirit, who is God's Spirit within us guiding and teaching us. Jesus was one fully God and fully man sinless as He walked this earth. His spirit and His authority can now be shared with everyone, no longer just within Him. Thank God for His finished work. He said greater the works are to be done because He was also bound by time and space and was one body while he walked this earth. Now, this same gift and power can spread to the whole world, with many having this one free gift.

    We are not intended to just be saved; we are intended to live in divine health and power and share it with others to receive the same thing. This gift of God is the only free gift there is ever. It is pure grace (unearned) and pure mercy (not receiving due punishment). It is the one free gift that keeps on giving. Stores or any kind of business says here is a free gift. If you have to give your personal information, it is not free. They will contact you without an invitation to buy something of theirs. You had to do something, give something that is personal first, and more is expected from you. Then they pressure or keep putting something in front of you until you give in and buy it. Free is something you receive without doing anything you do to earn it, something made available to you at no expense of any kind to you. You just get the blessing and the benefits of another's effort. That only comes through Jesus. Anything not supported by the foundation of Jesus will fail. It is an absolute.

Bring everything to the cross and place it at the feet of Jesus. We are to bring our problems to Him and not call them our problems anymore; they were dealt with at the cross. It is under His feet. Catch that. It is at His feet, conquered! We also will always know the way and the truth when we look to the cross. The cross is the picture of answered questions, truth, and solved problems. Look to the cross, and that is walking in faith and truth. God does not bring bad trials. He knows He cannot trust us, but He loves us anyway. He trusts Jesus, and Jesus already dealt with everything. It is not our great beauty and works today and Jesus's tomorrow. Jesus is the only source of beauty today, tomorrow, and forever.

God is so good. He sends a beautiful message in all things. Look at the word "your." What is in this word if you take off the "y"? Our! We are made to be part of "the our" that Jesus provided, which is an individual life changed by him to live life with Him. This life then becomes part of the body of Christ. It is ours to receive and work together for His purpose. If you look at the word "you" and take off the "y," you have the beginning of the word our. This is only part of the word "our" because until we have Jesus, there is something important missing in us. If you put the "y" on our, then it is "your," which simply means this: Jesus is "yours" if you will receive Him. He is for everyone—"ours." The "s" makes it more than one because He is for everyone. The "s" also represents having possession of because He is within us, ours, if we choose to invite Him. We were not made to live life alone. It starts with taking the "you" and wanting "our," which requires Him to get "your," which completes and gives the fulfillment that every person needs and looks for. Your true identity becomes yours and that is saved, redeemed, and empowered to what God always wanted for you. It is me and Jesus first, then others, and not just all about me or you. "You" is a lonely place brought by sin. Receiving "your" Savior is trusting He is "ours" that redeems, renews, and completes us all to make the body of Christ. See it.

Every religion just believing God exists, not being based on salvation through Jesus, or believing in other gods brings failure and emptiness. Praise God for the ones that bring to light that we need to accept Jesus to be saved. However, do you want to be saved and wasting away for heaven? Or do you want eternal life and all the blessings and benefits He provided to you now and forever? God does not give and take away. Yes, that is found in Job in the *Old Testament*. When Job's faith was high, it was good. When his faith was little, it was not. God's wrath against sin was present and had to be atoned because God is perfect and just, and sin is death and destruction. He cannot be amongst sin. Job just needed to trust in God, and that is it. When he did, he was blessed beyond measure. Trust God, not circumstances. The enemy cannot even pretend to have power when we just trust that God is only good. We have to choose to see it. We must have Jesus's finished work and focus on Him to trust. If we focus on self, we fall and get back up over and over only because of God's grace and mercy. The works of people will never be enough or complete because the source was first sinful. Things will come and go without Jesus because we cannot be our own savior. We can even think like we are saving ourselves by thinking it is our measure of faith in God that saves us. Jesus said faith the size of a mustard seed is enough. Take the hint: it is not about how much or little you do. Just believe in Him. God is not the author of your troubles. The devil is all about pride, which just leads to more and more sin.

Pride is sinful, and sin is the root of all evil. Our flesh is drawn to sin in this fallen world. Our flesh is still corrupted and can only be blessed with the finished work of Christ if we continue living by our spirit and renew our minds in God's Word. We have to continue letting our perfect spirit pour out into our soul and our flesh (our body). Our perfect born-again spirit wants our soul and body in the same goodness. Our soul is in the middle of our spirit and body. It can go either way. We have to choose to draw our soul (feelings, attitude, personality) in with our spirit and let Jesus finished work bless our soul and then our body with the same goodness that is in our spirit. God is a spirit, and our spirit is perfect, just like Jesus. If we invite the Holy Spirit to guide us, then we have Jesus and God's own Spirit guiding us. It does not get any more powerful than that because God is power. Our spirit will win over our flesh anytime, for our soul and our body will listen to our spirit before the world if we choose.

Everything responds to the power and authority that are in believers because Jesus provided this. His name alone is power and authority. Mindset is everything. We are to be set on the spirit and all good things and victory is ours to every part of ourselves in spirit, soul, and body. Then, we can spread this same goodness of Jesus to others. The flesh is drawn to sin and the first thing we can feel. However, the enemy lies and uses this. We must remember we always have a choice. Defeat is to think we do not and to be led by how we feel. If we simply do not go by what we feel like the enemy wants us to, and instead, we go by what we know, we will walk in the victory that is ours every time. It is that simple. We have it already. What our mind is stayed upon is where we will be. We cannot look around the world to see it yet until all is made new again. We have to see it inside us from our spirit. God wants us to use our imagination to see Him instead of pretending in fantasy, which leads to trouble and disappointment. One important thing we can do is teach this truth to others of all ages. We can spread the goodness of God just by sharing why we have the imagination to see Him. He is so good. He gives us our imagination to also use as a navigation system so we can move about in the world with ease if we so choose. We have to see it. Even if we are saved and try to see it from just our soul, we will live a great deal of time in disappointment and sad feelings. Our soul can only move toward good things if it is first guided by our born-again spirit. We see God and all good things from our spirit pouring into our souls. This is what it means to believe and see it with your whole heart.

When God's Word is shared, it is often from the Old Testament. The New Testament is the true gospel and the good news. We have the Old Testament to see and learn from. The New Testament is where we are to reside. Everything that is right and true points to Jesus, not the self. Psalms and Proverbs have some amazing words and are something I read often. However, remember the way David prayed is not how we are to pray. The saved have Jesus within us if we invite Him. We need not pray as if He is far away. He is as close as close can be. He is not even next to you but within you once you accept Him in your heart. Please also remember that we are not to worship or look to a pastor in a way that is only for Jesus. We follow Jesus only. A pastor or anyone in any position who is supposed to be sharing the good news of the gospel is a messenger, not our savior. They are other humans who need the finished work of Christ and also have to renew their minds just as everyone must.

"The plans of the diligent lead to profit as sure as haste leads to poverty" (Proverbs 21:5). If we hold tight to Jesus and look at what treasure really is, that is only the things He provided, we flourish.

Wanting our way now will always lead to loss and failure. What sounds like a good deal at your door now will not last. For example, an internet company comes to your front door with a high-speed internet service for a cheap price. Sounds great and sounds like a good thing at the moment. Well, yes, but in one year or even three months, that same service goes up, and then if you do not sign a contract for one year, you start seeing different fees that pop up on your bill and read that this discount is no longer effective. Then you have a bill that has gone up forty dollars or more for the exact same service. That is how it all works when it is not of the kingdom. Dishonesty and greed take effect.

God supplied the earth with everything that would be needed forever when He created the world in six days and rested on the seventh. He made everything to have life. Babies are life. He knew us before we were formed in our mother's womb (Jeremiah 1:5). Everything He created comes from a seed. We have free will to use that. We will not destroy the earth and use up everything, as the Bible clearly states in Revelation, that will not be done by man. I have been so blessed by reading Revelation. I used to be very afraid to read it and would not because of religion. It was not until I could see God without religion and know who Jesus is, know what He did for me, and what I have in me through Him that I could even begin to read. Religion teaches us works, and that brings fear. God loves us so much that he gave us His Word, the Bible, to read in its entirety as our instructions for living in this fallen world and receiving the door to Him so we are where we are supposed to be.

Personally, I have had plenty of years of experience in not getting where I should be, even moving backward because I was trying to do things on my own and even trying to help out God. All I ever needed to know was just to be loved by Him. Being in religion and even studying the Bible to where it is almost memorized is not it. The Bible is to be read from our spirit, not logic. Reading from our brain and not our spirit will lead to emptiness every time and even confusion if we do not just rest in Jesus and see Him in the scripture. We have all we will ever possibly need in Christ from the moment we receive Him. The walk is a time for us to be able to grasp His goodness. It is not about living in the Old Testament law. It is about living under grace, which is the new covenant that Jesus provided. "He has made us competent as ministers of a new covenant—not of the letter but of the Spirit; for the letter kills, but the Spirit gives life" (2 Corinthians 3:6). The letter is the written law that no one could keep. Sharing our Savior, Jesus Christ, who provided us with life all because of grace instead of law, is a must so many can be saved. We cannot save ourselves. Jesus makes us able, ready, and equipped to share His covenant of grace, which is the new covenant. It does not take a degree in theology to do this. It just takes knowing you are loved.

To truly have God's Word is for Him to have your heart. Jesus rests at the right hand of the Father because He gave us His perfect spirit that brought the Holy Spirit (God's Spirit) to guide us if we welcome Him to do so. We are ready and able to share. Are you willing? Jesus reconciled us back to our Heavenly Father God. All we have to do is, by faith, accept Jesus, and all of the goodness God originally planned for us becomes ours. God sees you like He sees Jesus. God loves you and sees no blemish, just righteousness and perfection. He is a spirit and is one with us in our perfect born-again spirit when we accept Jesus as our Savior and the finished work He provided.

Think about this: bees pollinate and spread good. They do a very important job. Do they even know what they or doing? No. They are just trying to get nectar and pollen for food to survive. Let us see the love of God and how He cares for them. Let us be usable like that. If a bee is cared for like that and can be used like that, we can do all things through Christ. God does not go by size, outward appearance, strength, age, or anything else that the world goes by.

He uses anyone who is willing, and it is He who gets the glory. I pray we let the Lord work through us and that we know we do not need to try and help Him out. More is accomplished when we rest in Him and just be loved. Remember, we have everything in Christ because of grace. It is free and not earned by you or me. Jesus died and rose again on the third day because of His love for us. If we focus on grace, we live loved, and we rest. Jesus changes our nature when we accept His perfect spirit to be ours. Our spirit is no longer corrupted and sinful. It is righteous and full of life. We turn from sin because we have a new drawing near God's righteous nature in our spirit. We will remember why we have all of this just given to us if we simply believe in Jesus and not ourselves. It is all because of grace. We are loved that much. God's grace changes everything every time.

Thank Him

Thank God for His love. Thank Him for Jesus, the best friend we could ever have. To stay on the right path requires living under grace and living in appreciation, not circumstances. Trust Him, and see His promises in your heart. Logic will never work. It is too small for God and His abilities. Living thankful is the key to receiving everything Jesus provided to all of us. We praise God when we live in appreciation of Him. I tell my children often the key is to live in thankfulness and appreciation not circumstances. If we are not seeking a place of appreciation, then we are automatically falling into circumstances. We remember who He is and what we have in Jesus when we live every day, thankful for what God gave us and for what Jesus did for us, not just on the Christmas and Easter holidays.

There was a storm that came through in the very early morning hours. We were all still asleep. My husband smelled something burning and woke me up. Lightning had caused the power to surge, and our camera system was burning up. At first, we did not know where the smell was coming from. The smell subsided, so we thought everything was fine. We looked, and the camera system had smoke coming from it. So, we were able to get it unplugged and out of the house. My son looked at me and said, "I see that it is important to live thankful." We were in the right place at the right time. That is what God does. He does not bring bad weather. He brings safety and puts you in the right place at the right time. It is a choice, choose life.

Remember you are a whosoever. There may be 1,000 books like this. Well, let this be 1,001 because I am a whosoever, and so are you. If one life is changed because we let the Lord work through us, glory to God forever, and amen! The goal is to show you, not tell you. We do not have to have a terrible experience or bad life to find Jesus. God would never plan or want bad for us. The same one true God would not send us problems and then send His only Son, Jesus, to fix our problems. I was taught that God does plan bad for us and that we are just supposed to trust in that. No, Jesus had it bad and took the bad on Himself. It is not for us; He did it. Jesus came and saved us because of God's grace toward us. We need to share the truth and not be afraid of how we look or someone's reaction or if they think we are out of our minds. I try to be out of my mind—praise God. I desire to be in the spirit that Jesus gave me. I am focused on Jesus, not myself, and choosing to reside and live from my spirit. Yes, I waver. I grow closer to God and grow to let more of my just-like Jesus spirit pour into my soul and body no matter what, all because of grace. It is about Jesus, not me. I cannot lose what He already gave me. He died once and saved me once and for all.

Glory to God always. Even when I mess up and get on myself again, I am covered and always close to God. It is the motive and awareness of our heart, not the action, that God cares about most. We are to live boldly, expecting good, not bad. There is godly boldness and expectation and worldly boldness and expectation. The difference is the right one is about Christ, and the worldly one is about self and pride that always leads to destruction every time. Our identity is in Christ, not problems. Let us be aware of the goodness of God, not problems. Let us expect health, prosperity, and blessing, not sickness, poverty, and death. The devil wants us offended and thinking we are better than someone else so he can get us alone. He uses both. Both are about self, whether it is that one thinks that they are better than others or not good enough. Being about self and alone is a weakness that the enemy preys upon. Remember, he is already a defeated foe. He has no power if you do not falsely or erroneously give it to him.

One of the things we worry about most in this world is our children. Trust God with your children. When I first got to know Jesus, I was still thinking I had to do instead of trust and rest. I took on trying to protect them from everything myself. This cannot be done. Just as I am covered by the blood of Jesus, so are my children. When we trust Him with our children, it is amazing how not only you but the whole family will flourish in the blink of an eye. Also, just as it is not about your works, it is not about your children's works either. Just as we rest in Jesus and things just flow wonderfully, if we teach them to rest in Him, the same will go for them. Rest. All the good comes from what Jesus did, not what you do. The best moments are when you blink and think, *Wow! How did this happen?* Guess how? Jesus! You know what just happened; you rested in Jesus. Praise God! Let us keep in rest, not works.

His Word will absolutely never return void, and there is no painful toil when it is God. Let us build up the body of Christ and move and share, supporting one another, not clicking up with people who we think are the same as us in some way. Thinking we are like someone else, or they are like us, is all a lie. We are not to want to be like anyone else or follow anyone else besides Jesus. Otherwise, we put people before God. Finding comfort in the lie we are like someone else or doing like someone else will always lead to a fall if it is not based on Jesus. The only thing that is truly identical here on earth or in heaven is a born-again believer's spirit is identical to Jesus's spirit. Believers in Christ all have Jesus's shared spirit that gave their spirit new birth, new life. This is the only thing that is the same as someone else, and it always starts with Jesus. Being one in spirit with Jesus and other believers is what makes up the body of Christ. Jesus is the only true union that will last forever.

God loves us all and is not willing for any to not be with Him. God says whosoever or whoever. That means all. He also plainly tells us it is all about the heart of someone (1 Samuel 16:7). Even Jesus's heritage was traced back to Noah's son Shem. God left nothing for us to be confused about. He says seek, and you will find. He will even bless you and protect you if you are seeking a place He would rather you not because He is grace and mercy. He has done this for me over and over. If one looks at even the lineage of Jesus coming to be born, it goes back to Shem. Catch this: Noah means rest, and Shem means name. Rest in His name. Wow! God showed that all redemption, authority, and power are in the name of Jesus and the motivation of a person's heart in every way and in every aspect must be Jesus. It was not about the outward appearance of Jesus, what He had, or where He lived as a child. No one would have known He was Lord from these things. He was known by His heart!

Life is not about prestige, who you are, or what you do. Prestige is not God. He purposely lowered Himself so we could be lifted up. All He wants from us is to know He loves us. He wants us to believe in His only Son who suffered for you and me. If who you are is not found in Jesus, then you have not even met yourself yet, much less anyone else. There are plenty of us acting who are not actors by trade. Life is only life when we die to ourselves and just rest in Jesus. Just being a doctor, lawyer, famous anything, artist, or anything else without Jesus's full gift of grace is not it. All this will pass away, and catch it: many of the considered great jobs will have no place in the new heaven or new earth. There will be no problems, no arguments, no disease, and everything will be beautiful art already created. We must see things from the forever perspective (the kingdom). Yes, those jobs could be used for God's glory now to show who He is and His coming kingdom. The problem is that is not always the case. The only true kingdom is God's kingdom.

The thing that will matter is the lives we touched by being usable for God and the lives that were saved because they knew of and accepted Jesus. That will have eternal value. Again, He is not willing that any should perish (2 Peter 3:8). People who do not know and look to what career they will have to define success or find life are people who I hear cannot wait to retire or they are completely changing careers. Seeking Him and His guidance is the only way to peace and success. If one is called to be a doctor, do it for the kingdom, and good will happen. God is merciful and knows not all know or believe Jesus is the Healer. That is why He gave us doctors who used to have a heart for service and would even make house calls. Things not based on Jesus fall every time. If the glory does not go to God, it is not Him and, therefore, is the wrong thing to be doing. For example, there are many people going to college now who have so much debt when they finish that it weighs on them tremendously. That is not God. God makes all crooked paths straight; if it is God and not self, doors will open that no one can explain because of grace. He said time and again that the Israelites did not want a king appointed from among the people. They would not listen. The only true king is Jesus. The only one who is ever heard of to have shed His own blood for His people to have the kingdom is Jesus. He did not run, even in torment. He stayed and finished it! God's will brings peace always.

Just Be Loved

Be loved. The only way to live in what Jesus provided for us is to live loved. Then, good things happen. He loves you more than you ever think of being loved. It is not about how much you know or how much you do not know. Just know He loves you. To live a life dedicated to the finished work of Christ is to know He is love. God loves you no matter what. He loves you in your successes, and He loves you in times of trouble. He does not just love us in defeat. Unfortunately, this is usually when we will be willing to look to Him. That is not God's plan.

We suffer needlessly because we think love is earned because of what sin did. Sin brought punishment. Since we still live in a sinful, fallen world, if we think from our flesh and not our spirit, we still think we are to be punished and have to earn something through painful toil. We should not settle for that. It is equally important to realize we must not have it all figured out. We are to rely on the Holy Spirit's guidance, not ourselves. We should not go by what we feel. We must go by what we know in our spirit and not our flesh. We were made to rely on God and Him alone. The world is still fallen; the believer in Christ is not. We are always protected and will be where we are supposed to be with the guidance of the Holy Spirit. We will live in love no matter what is going on around us. The key is to choose an attitude and posture of rest, "just be." We are to just be loved. Anything else is our flesh still trying to dominate us and focus on punishment and works instead of just love. Our spirit will never try to dominate because it is pure and righteous; it is a choice because free will is love.

Remember holidays like Christmas and Easter are extra time set aside to appreciate what Jesus did for us. It is not even about when because we do not know exactly when either one occurred. If the Bible does not tell us, that is the important clue. This means that is not what we are to focus on. We should live in this appreciation daily. Traditions are not bad in the right place, like families doing certain activities at special times. That can be fun and exciting and is good in its place. It is Jesus first, and a relationship with Him is not to be religious, repetitive actions, or traditions. That is empty. This does not reach God. We cannot continue celebrating Christmas and Easter as the world has made them to be about a man in a red suit and a bunny with eggs. Christmas is supposed to be about Jesus's birth. Easter is when Jesus died, rose again on the third day, and set us free from sin and death. Let us share the truth so others can have Christ and win. He is the one true victory, and wow, we did not have to do anything to earn this. We just trust in what He has done.

Remember, God is not sending us bad weather, plagues, or any other problems. We live in a fallen world where sin still exists. It has all been paid for and redemption provided by Jesus, but sin has not been completely destroyed yet. Sin can only cease to exist by starting brand new because anything righteous can only be built on truth in God's Word and cannot be where sin is and still be truth. Sin brings death and destruction, like bad weather and plagues. It brings punishment and problems. God brings love, grace, and righteousness through Jesus. Sin has all been atoned for through Jesus. God's wrath against sin is over because of His Son. One day, the new heaven and new earth will come, and there will be no trace of sin anywhere. The only way for sin to not exist anywhere is to start over because perfection cannot be perfection where sin exists. This new beginning has already begun. It started with Jesus coming and atoning for sin once and for all. He provided a new birth for all people to be born again with His perfect shared spirit and to be reunited with God. This is where we are right now. We are to be sharing the good news of the gospel that is grace because of Jesus so that everyone has a chance to be saved. Once the gospel has been spread all over the world, giving all people a chance to choose Jesus, then the end of this fallen world will come. Sin will be gone forever. Then the new heaven and the new earth will be, and we will live in perfection with our Perfect Father and in our glorified bodies forever.

The enemy uses what we do not know. God wants more good for you than you could ever imagine or want. Things seem to take time in the physical only because God is merciful and knows we cannot handle His goodness all at once. This is because our flesh is not full of righteousness like our spirit. We have to see it in our hearts first because we do not have our glorified bodies yet. He is not willing that the blessing becomes a curse to someone who does not choose to receive the goodness of the blessing. Simply, God and His Word are what we are to stand on no matter what we see or no matter what other circumstances we have around us. His Word is true, and what His Word says will come to be every single time. If we are trying to figure out something that He has not revealed to us, we are not resting and trusting. We are not to have to know and understand things that are only for God right now because He is grace and mercy. We should not try to be God or take His place, even accidentally. We were made in His image and likeness and to rely on Him. We are not to try to do what only He is meant to do. Just as I should not try to build a house on my own when I do not know how or ask someone to cook a dish themselves that only I have the recipe for. We are to stand on God's Word and not try to get answers that we cannot, should not, or could not handle. God is not secretive; He is protective.

When we receive our glorified bodies that are only focused on our righteous spirit, then we will know and can handle all things. For now, we wait by faith because the saved have their spirit just like Jesus and flesh that was born into sin and is still around sin. Perfection cannot exist with sin. There has to be a barrier or the whole thing becomes bad and will fall. Everything stands on God's Word. His Word is perfection and cannot exist with sin. This is why we live by faith through our spirit that flows one way out to our soul, body, and others so our perfect spirit does not come in contact with sin and no longer would be righteous. Faith is our protection, trust in Jesus, and our rest in God. Just be loved and live by faith.

Receiving our glorified bodies is the final piece of what Jesus provided for us. For now, we have our perfect, glorified spirit to live by on this earth until Jesus comes back. The walk on this earth is the renewing of mind to what we now have in Christ, using it, and sharing it. When Jesus returns, we receive the last piece, our glorified bodies. It is amazing how God made us in His image. He has three parts: Father, Son, and Holy Spirit. He gave us three parts: spirit, soul, and body. God made everything so easy. It is us that make things so hard. Even after sin entered the world, He gave us a way. We need Jesus, the one and only Savior. Living loved is how we walk with Jesus. He loves you and me. Jesus died on the cross between two thieves. One believed in Him and is with Him now. This man did wrong and was on the cross for his crimes. This is something to pay attention to as everything represents God reaching out to us with open arms; the thief was literally dying when he found Jesus. All because he believed in Him, this man did not perish and saw eternal life. Until the last moments of his life, he did not do right. The best thing he ever did was accept Jesus. Catch that!

I have been asked so many times in my life if I am religious or not. I came to understand that many people ask that question thinking the answer means if one believes in God or not. This is a big deal because if that is all someone knows or thinks that they need, they are not heaven-bound. God and religion do not go together. We should be concerned with whether someone is a believer who has accepted Jesus yet or not. When I became aware of why I kept being asked only if I was religious, I remembered I used to think that same way or ask the same thing because I only knew religion, not God. Truly, I had forgotten I used to do this because that seemed like a life that was not even real, just a nightmare that I woke up from. At one time, I did think religion and God went together and that I had to follow some religious practices to hope I reached God and would see heaven one day. Religion is not God, and so it is not love. It is empty and hopeless and does not connect us to Him. It distracts us from focusing only on Jesus. We are to be believers in Jesus Christ, our one and only Savior forever. He connects us back to God, where we are simply to be loved by Him. From there, our walk is not works and good deeds. It is sharing the love of Jesus with others. He is the door to the love of God. We are not to try to love God ourselves. We were not created to do that, and we could not if we tried because we were born with a corrupted spirit because of sin. This brings separation and resentment to God. When we accept Jesus, we are also saying I love You to God by our faith. To receive goodness and to expect goodness is our love for God. This is a love back to Him that does nothing but fill us. That is what God wants. He just wants to fill us with His love, not for us to try to love Him. God loves us that much.

Trying to get God to love you will exhaust you. I have been there. He made things the opposite way. We were created to first be loved by Him. Knowing He loves us is faith. Our faith is what is love back to God, not our works. We are to receive the kingdom like a child with an open heart. "Truly I tell you, anyone who will not receive the kingdom of God like a little child will never enter it" (Luke 18:17). It is sad to think that there are people I have known who I do not know if they are with the Lord. They either had been in religion believing in God and not accepting Jesus or worshiping false gods throughout their lives. Let us share so this does not continue to happen. God is not willing that any should perish and not be with Him. "The Lord is not slow in keeping his promise, as some understand slowness. Instead he is patient with you, not wanting anyone to perish, but everyone to come to repentance" (2 Peter 3:9). You must know you are loved. We have a choice. I choose to be a vessel with the valve on. Will you?

Scars only come from living life on our own. The only one with scars forever is Jesus. He has scars on His glorified body because God is truth and cannot lie or everything would fall. The truth is there had to be an atonement for sin, one perfect sacrifice that brought our redemption and reunion back to our Heavenly Father, who is God. He cannot and will not deny that truth and that it happened. Jesus is the only one to still have scars that point to the victory at the cross. Let us not embrace the struggle. Let us hold to the victory that is ours in Christ forever, once and for all. We are to come boldly and expecting to God because of what Jesus did for us. We are only to expect from God, not people. If we do this, we will never again be disappointed. We should always meet people where they are in love. Remember, we must accept Jesus to be saved. We must also invite the Holy Spirit to guide our lives so we are not just converted to righteousness instead of sin and death; we are also to be producing spiritual fruit now. Yes, that is an amazing gift. To love God is to first be loved and, through faith, receive all that Jesus provided, not just one part. God wants you to enjoy life to the fullest forever. He wants us all to enjoy being in community with others, not in fear or pride in all its forms. He does not want us in pride boasting or in pride being shy and not wanting to talk for fear of judgment by others. We do not need to wait for God to show up. That is Old Testament mentality. We are in the New Testament, the new covenant of grace, not law. He is already within those who accept Jesus and is available to those who have not yet. He wants you to have it all. The only way to be a disciple, one who follows the Teacher, is to invite the Holy Spirit to guide your life after you accept Christ as your Savior. Then, you receive the whole gift in its entirety. It is all this simple: just be loved. To Him be the glory forever. Welcome.

Invitation

Receive Jesus as Your Savior:

Believe (trust) in this with all of your heart and confess (say) it with your mouth.

I am a sinner. I want to turn away from sin. I need a Savior that is only found in You, Jesus. I believe You were born and died, and God raised You from the dead on the third day. I believe You delivered me from sin and death. Jesus, You are alive. I believe You are seated at the right hand of the Father. I receive You and Your perfect spirit to make my spirit brand-new, perfect, and righteous and the opportunity to have God's Spirit guide my life. I make You my Lord and Savior once and for all. I am Yours, Jesus. I receive the perfect born-again spirit that You have provided to me. I am no longer a sinner. I am Yours, and You are mine. I am the righteousness of God in Christ.

Invite the Holy Spirit to Guide Your Life:

I welcome the Holy Spirit to guide my life. I desire God's guidance and plan for my life, not my own. I am Yours, and You are mine through Jesus.

If you declare with your mouth, "Jesus is Lord," and believe in your heart that God raised him from the dead, you will be saved. For it is with your heart that you believe and are justified, and it is with your mouth that you profess your faith and are saved. As Scripture says, "Anyone who believes in him will never be put to shame." For there is no difference between Jew and Gentile—the same Lord is Lord of all and richly blesses all who call on him, for, "Everyone who calls on the name of the Lord will be saved."

Romans 10:9–13

See, it is not about how you start. It is about how you finish. All that matters is you now have the victory. This is your true beginning. Welcome to eternal life and abundance. Praise God!

Printed in the USA
CPSIA information can be obtained
at www.ICGtesting.com
LVHW020801091124
796100LV00002B/212